Ending ESG
and Restoring
the Economic
Enlightenment

Ending ESG and Restoring the Economic Enlightenment

Edited by
Phil Gramm and
Terrence Keeley

AEI Press

Publisher for the American Enterprise Institute
WASHINGTON, DC

ISBN-13: 978-0-8447-5073-6 (Paperback)

Library of Congress Control Number: 2024936279

AEI PRESS

Publisher for the American Enterprise Institute
for Public Policy Research
1789 Massachusetts Avenue, NW
Washington, DC 20036
www.aei.org

Printed in the United States of America

Contents

Introduction

Phil Gramm and Terrence Keeley

The modern-day phenomenon that has become known as environmental, social, and governance (ESG) investing did not spontaneously generate, nor was it hewn into stone tablets and handed to Moses on Mount Sinai. Rather, its incarnation is entirely attributable to the United Nations. More specifically, ESG traces its lineage to the UN's 1948 Universal Declaration of Human Rights, as well as the declaration's later, more programmatic iterations, the UN's Millennium Development Goals and Sustainable Development Goals.

That the Universal Declaration was adopted while the globe was reeling in the aftermath of World War II and the UN was still in its formative stages speaks volumes about the formidable influence that Eleanor Roosevelt and the United States had on the UN's proceedings. At a time when Europe and Japan had no hope or implementable plans for their reconstruction, the declaration defined an aspirational political, social, and economic agenda that was intentionally utopian.

Among other things, the declaration proclaimed that "the inherent dignity and . . . equal and inalienable rights of all members of the human family is the foundation of freedom, justice and peace in the world."[1] It also stipulated that every human being is entitled to employment, social security, equal pay, the right to rest and leisure, a living wage, free education, and full artistic expression. Its detailed text makes plain that so-called universal living wages must be sufficient for housing, food, clothing, medical care, paid vacation, and a comfortable retirement.

As you might expect, India led objections from the developing world to all these aspirations, knowing in 1946 that it could not fulfill a single one. But of course, no country in the world could meet all these objectives in 1946. Indeed, no country is meeting them today.

Fast-forward to the present, and you begin to appreciate the astounding power of economic growth over the postwar period. Economic advancements over the past 75 years exceeded anything that World War II's victors ever imagined possible. ESG cannot be understood independent of this unimaginable economic progress fueled by the expansion of market-based economies and the explosion of world trade, which made it possible for the United Nations to attempt to channel that cornucopia of progress to achieve its social goals.

As Figure 1 shows, until recently, more than half of humanity lived in extreme poverty. As recently as 1975, one out of every two human beings lived on less than $1.91 a day (adjusted for inflation), the official World Bank definition for abject poverty. After Ronald Reagan and Margaret Thatcher sparked a renewed commitment to market-based capitalism and a vast expansion of global trade, humanity's stultifying poverty numbers began to decline sharply. The General Agreement on Tariffs and Trade, the World Trade Organization, the European Union, and the negotiation of numerous regional free trade agreements allowed the volume of world trade to soar 4,500 percent since 1950.[2] Genetic engineering produced a new agricultural revolution, and modern mechanization and computerization caused industrial production to surge first in the developed world and then worldwide. Hundreds of millions of Chinese citizens living in abject poverty escaped rancid squalor and ill health only after Deng Xiaoping ordered his Communist Party to embrace a more market-based economic system.

The results have been astounding: From 1990 until 2020, 128,000 people escaped abject poverty *every day*. Today, fewer than one in 10 human beings live in abject poverty.

Figure 1. Percentage of the World Population Living in Extreme Poverty, 1945–2018

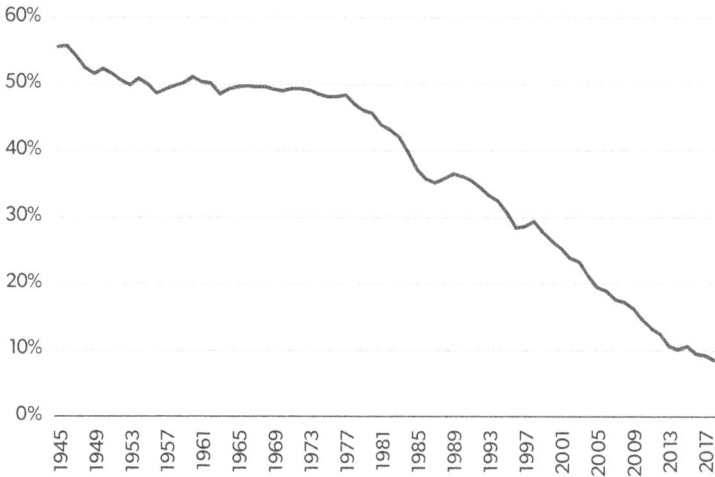

Source: Adapted from Michail Moatsos, "Global Extreme Poverty: Present and Past Since 1820," in *How Was Life? Volume II: New Perspectives on Well-Being and Global Inequality Since 1820* (Organisation for Economic Co-operation and Development, 2021), https://www.oecd-ilibrary.org/sites/e20f2f1a-en/index.html?itemId=/content/component/e20f2f1a-en#wrapper.

Against this astonishingly positive economic backdrop and the growing promise of the new millennium, the United Nations turned its attention from reducing world poverty to directing the fruits of economic growth to a broad array of social objectives. To address this new opportunity, the United Nations gathered the largest assembly of national leaders in history. In early September 2000, 100 heads of state, 47 heads of government, three monarchs, and 8,000 other ministers and international leaders representing more than 150 countries gathered at the UN headquarters in New York City. This deliberative body ultimately adopted a collection of Millennium Development Goals that triumphantly reaffirmed the Universal Declaration's principles and objectives.

To the goals mentioned in the original declaration, UN negotiators added disarmament, respect for nature, and multiple relief measures for Africa. Specifically, 150 national leaders committed themselves to eight goals, all to be achieved by 2015. The goals were:

1. The complete eradication of poverty and hunger;

2. Universal primary education;

3. Greater gender equality;

4. Reduced child mortality;

5. Improved maternal health;

6. The end of HIV/AIDS, malaria, and other diseases;

7. Environmental sustainability; and

8. A global partnership for development.

It was during these first years of the new millennium when the foundations of the modern ESG movement were set into place. In 2005, as an integrated part of all these newly ambitious development objectives, UN Secretary-General Kofi Annan tasked a group of international investors to generate new principles for investing that might somehow accelerate the attainment of the UN's evolving and increasingly ambitious economic, social, and environmental goals. Annan's expert financial group included representatives of the pension, investment, and banking industries from 12 countries and a 70-person assembly of supplemental experts from every continent. Once the right investment principles were formed, Annan and his appointees presumed, they would be put to practical use, positively transforming the globe. With the right investment principles, private finance could also play a far more prominent role in advancing the UN's agenda.

In April 2006, after 12 months of deliberations, Annan's hand-picked officials launched their Principles for Responsible Investment at the New York Stock Exchange. Secretary-General Annan himself rang the bell.

Today, six UN-sanctioned Principles for Responsible Investment form the theoretical basis for all global initiatives relating to ESG investing. Just like the UN's Universal Declaration and its ever-evolving development goals, these principles were aspirational and intended to be voluntary. Specifically, signatories pledged to:

1. Incorporate ESG issues into all investment analysis and decision-making processes;

2. Be active owners, integrating ESG issues into all ownership policies and practices;

3. Seek appropriate disclosures on ESG issues through the entities in which they invest;

4. Promote acceptance and implementation of the principles in the investment industry;

5. Work together to enhance effectiveness in implementing the principles; and

6. Report on all activities and progress toward implementing the principles.

The original responsible-investment statement also offered an intentionally non-exhaustive list of ESG objectives of specific concern for all signatories, as shown in Table 1.

Table 1. UN Principles for Responsible Investment: Original List of Material ESG Risks

Environmental	Social	Governance
• Climate change	• Human rights	• Bribery and corruption
• Resource depletion	• Modern slavery	
• Waste	• Child labor	• Executive pay
• Pollution	• Working conditions	• Board diversity and structure
• Deforestation	• Employee relations	• Political lobbying and donations
		• Tax strategy

Source: UN Principles for Responsible Investment, website, https://www.unpri. org.

To the extent any of these issues constitute material financial risks, ESG investment products and methodologies were intended to eliminate them or reprice them accordingly. However, because of overreliance on divestment rather than investment, ESG in practice has failed at remediating any of these concerns meaningfully.

As of the first quarter of 2023, the UN's Principles for Responsible Investment initiative had 5,381 signatories. Collectively, these institutions oversee more than $120 trillion in assets.[33] This makes the UN's investment pledge by far the largest in history. According to its website, "Investors have a critical role to play in addressing the issues that the world is facing."[4]

As you would expect, the asset-management industry actively positioned itself for the inevitable capital flows that such a widespread convergence of conviction might generate. American financial services firm Morningstar now tracks more than 600 ESG-themed funds alone. In 2021, broadly defined ESG-themed exchange-traded funds, separate accounts, and other investment strategies attracted more than $8 billion of new assets every day.[5]

In addition to ESG investment principles and products, advocates and activists have pressed for adopting ESG goals in corporate shareholder and board meetings. Similarly, sympathetic governments now actively promote ESG goals using expanded regulatory powers. As ESG's momentum has swelled, these regulations have become more coercive.

California and the EU plan to force all corporations with more than $1 billion in revenues to report their carbon emissions.[6] To fund ESG goals through the investment of private retirement savings, President Joe Biden's Department of Labor altered the obligation set out in the 1974 Employee Retirement Income Security Act (ERISA) for investments to be made by fiduciaries "solely in the interest of" and for the "exclusive purpose of providing benefits" to the investor.[7] Even though Biden's CHIPS and Science Act never mentions environmental or social inclusivity concerns, ESG dictates have been required in the law's regulatory implementation, suggesting multiple ESG coercions may become standard additions in the future implementation of any new federal programs.

As if on cue, the Securities and Exchange Commission (SEC) has also now proposed new regulations that will force every public company to build climate risk into its business plans, production processes, and supply chains. While the requirement would apply only to large companies, the regulations would in the process force environmental requirements onto hundreds of thousands of small companies that supply inputs and services to large companies. In short, the private economy is increasingly being coerced into meeting a growing number of environmental and social goals that Congress never mandated.

ESG coercions have not been confined to public policy, however. In recent years, index fund managers have exercised the voting power of shares that belong to their clients to promote a growing array of ESG goals. This action is a clear violation of the offending managers' fiduciary responsibility; the managers are voting shares they do not own without notifying owners of the potential impact of their actions and without getting the owners' permission to vote their shares in ways that may not be in the owners' economic interest. Such actions by investment managers are also a threat to corporate leaders who are trying to operate their companies in the long-run financial interest of their shareowners. Governmental efforts to dilute fiduciary rules that were put in place to protect the financial interests of small investors further aid and abet this process. Increasingly, large index managers are supplanting the roles democratically accountable agencies are supposed to play by imposing their own environmental and social agendas at the financial expense of their clients, in whose sole interests they are legally required to serve.

The ESG agenda has now become a political movement with ambitions to empower other claimants against businesses and the investors who own them. For instance, Sens. Bernie Sanders (I-VT) and Elizabeth Warren (D-MA) have recently tried to induce BlackRock, one of the world's largest private investment firms, to use its share-voting power to force private companies to yield to union demands.

Sen. Warren also introduced the Accountable Capitalism Act, which would force large American companies to acquire a new federal charter under which they would have obligations to not just their shareholders but multiple "stakeholders," including the general public, the workforce, the community, the environment, and additional societal factors.[8] Sen. Warren's bill would further mandate that employees of large public companies elect 40 percent of the company's board members. A new, virtually omnipotent Office of US Corporations would decide whether the requirements of the Accountable Capitalism Act were being met. Only after they are met would investors receive whatever return is left on the investments and companies they in fact own. Moreover, stakeholders who claim that their interests have not been sufficiently served would be empowered to sue the company.

The net result of the Warren bill would be to eliminate private companies' fiduciary duty to serve the long-run financial interests of investors, forcing them to serve the interests of stakeholders, none of whom have a legal stake in the company. The passage of this bill would represent the largest government intrusion into private commercial activity in American history and profoundly affect the market value of every major company in the country.

As if to announce step two of the Warren plan, the UK Labour Party now proposes to go beyond board-seat meddling, requiring that employees receive a 10 percent ownership stake in every major British corporation.[9] Back in the US, Sens. Chuck Schumer (D-NY) and Sanders want to block corporate stock buybacks and possibly halt dividend payments to investors—including retirement funds—unless companies pay additional benefits to workers as well.[10]

All of these efforts directly contravene the principles and practices that have made centuries of human flourishing possible. They harken back to an ancient time, when economies were moribund and poverty never-ending. It is worth reflecting on these ancient times so we do not return to them.

The Enlightenment and Subsequent Explosion of Human Well-Being

For most of human history, workers and savers were constrained by communal institutions such as the tribe and the village. Their return for work and thrift was subject to communal sharing, and therefore, the incentive to exert effort and forgo consumption was diminished.

The last era dominated by communal interest was the feudalistic world of the Middle Ages. The worker, who was often little more than a serf or a peasant, owed fealty to the king, the church, the village, and the guild. In this world of communal sharing, the reward for exerting effort was so plundered that for over a thousand years—from the fall of the Roman Empire to the Enlightenment of the 18th century—little significant economic growth occurred.

Economic historian Gregory Clark has compared wages in England over 600 years and found no significant increases except for short periods when events such as the Black Death significantly reduced the supply of labor and temporarily increased wages. All of that changed with the Enlightenment and the Industrial Revolution that it fostered.[11]

The 18th-century Enlightenment liberated mind, soul, and property, empowering ordinary people to think their own thoughts, worship God in their own way, and benefit from the fruits of their own labor and thrift. Under the feudal system of the Middle Ages, the crown, the church, the village, and the guild had often become leeches that drained away the incentive to work and save. After the Enlightenment, ordinary people came to own their own labor and the fruits of their own thrift as a property right.

This became a fundamental and world-changing principle, unleashing explosions in work, thrift, and innovation that had never before been seen in world history. As the Enlightenment economist Adam Smith put it, "The property which every man has in his own labour, as it is the original foundation of all other property, so it is the most sacred and inviolable."[12] This quote is carved into Smith's gravestone, an indication of its presumed importance.

As labor and capital came to serve their owner—not the crown, the church, the village, or the guild—economies began to awaken from a thousand years of stagnation. The British Parliament stripped away the leeching influence of royal charters and initiated reforms that ultimately allowed businesses to incorporate simply by meeting preset capital requirements. Of equal importance, Parliament established the principle that laws created in a process of open deliberation, not the leeching influence and rampant cronyism that dominated the medieval marketplace, would govern business. The explosion of knowledge and production that drives human flourishing to this day was born via the Enlightenment principle that established labor and capital as private property, not communal property subject to involuntary sharing.

The extraordinary energy released by the Enlightenment was followed by the Industrial Revolution, which began in Britain and spread to continental Europe and North America. While poets, philosophers, and many historians have viewed the Industrial Revolution as a period of extraordinary poverty and labor exploitation, that description doesn't reflect the historical evidence.

In rural Britain, the poor were largely out of sight. Run-down mud huts when viewed from the veranda of the manor house across the creek appeared quaint. But when poor people rushed into the cities to take industrial jobs, they suddenly became visible. Poets and authors extolled rural life and lamented its passing. But the millions of poor people who chose to leave rural Britain and flood into the cities did so because they were looking for a better life.

By every available economic measure, they found it. Wages suddenly exploded. The real wages of skilled workers—which had been largely unchanged for 600 years—rose by 113 percent from 1840 to 1900, and the real wages of their unskilled helpers rose by 124 percent over the same period.[13] In England, real wages measured in 1980 dollars rose from less than $500 per year in 1830 to over $1,200 in 1900.[14]

But monetary and quantitative measures aren't the only things that improved; in succession, nonmonetary life measures improved dramatically too. Life expectancy rose by 22 percent.[15] British literacy rates rose from 64 percent for men and 53 percent for women in 1830 to an almost universal 98 percent for both by 1900. An index for the quality of life for Victorian children—which combined metrics of mortality rates in the first five years of life, a body mass index to measure adequate nutrition, a wage index, school enrollment, and female literacy—more than doubled from 40.9 in 1840 to 93.5 in 1900 (measured against a level of 100, set in 1914).[16] Financial progress underwrote improved living standards. The same thing happened in America. Between 1870 and 1900, America's real gross national product (GNP) exploded by 233 percent. While the population nearly doubled, real per capita GNP surged by 90 percent. Real wages of nonfarm employees grew by 53 percent, and staples of life such as food, clothing, and shelter became more plentiful, their prices falling on average by more than 50 percent. The illiteracy rate plunged by 46 percent, and life expectancy increased by 12.5 percent.[17]

By any objective measure, a new era of human achievement had begun—and this astounding progress has never ended. Private property, market-driven economies, and world trade accomplished something no benevolent king's redistribution, no loving bishop's charity, no mercantilist advocate of protectionism, and no powerful guild's exclusion of competitors ever accomplished. It delivered broad-based, unprecedented prosperity.

Figure 2 shows the extraordinary explosion of world per capita gross domestic product in constant dollars that the Enlightenment and the Industrial Revolution ignited. The growth of per capita income is all the more astonishing when you realize that the population grew tenfold between 1700 and 2000.

Capitalism's most famous antagonist, Karl Marx, saw what many philosophers and historians failed to see: The Industrial Revolution achieved "more massive and more colossal productive force than have all preceding generations together," all in a span of a "scarce one hundred years."[18] Based on the erroneous notion that all value came exclusively from labor, Marx assumed that the financier, entrepreneur, and manager were non-contributing claimants on the fruits of the workers' labor and that government could displace them and then "wither away" as growth occurred spontaneously. In Marx's utopian world, workers would receive all value created in society automatically, benevolently, and in perpetuity.

Figure 2. Inflation-Adjusted Gross Domestic Product per Capita Income Growth Since the Year 1000

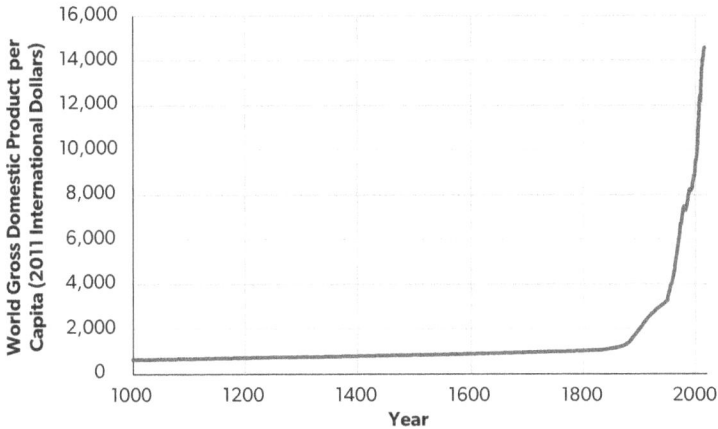

Note: An international dollar is a measure of purchasing power equivalent to what a dollar would buy in the United States.

Source: E. Kwan Choi, "Per Capita Income in World History," https://www2. econ.iastate.edu/classes/econ355/choi/rankh.htm; University of Groningen, Maddison Project Database, version 2018, https://www.rug.nl/ggdc/ historicaldevelopment/maddison/releases/maddison-project-database-2018?lang=en; and Jutta Bolt et al., "Rebasing 'Maddison': New Income Comparisons and the Shape of Long-Run Economic Development" (working paper, Maddison Project, Groningen, Netherlands, January 2018), https://www.rug. nl/ggdc/html_publications/memorandum/gd174.pdf.

But as we know too well from the brutal lessons of history, no government has ever been able to replicate the efficiency and innovation of private finance and entrepreneurialism. Once states began usurping total control of the market, it was only prosperity and freedom that withered away, not government.

Amid the recorded successes of capitalism and failures of socialism rooted in Marxism, pre-Enlightenment socialism has effectively been reincarnated in the name of ESG and stakeholder capitalism. When politicians say that the owner of a business did not build that business, they are espousing the same socialism that defined the Middle Ages. They are in essence saying labor and thrift do not belong to individuals but rather to society as a whole since the social structure in which businesses were built was a necessary part of their success.

Most business owners would respond that, while they surely benefited from government laws and courts, as well as from roads, schools, police protection, and other public services, they paid their fair share of taxes to fund each of these services as their businesses expanded. But for their businesses, far fewer roads and schools would have been built. All public services are ultimately funded by private enterprise.

Because our living memory of the failure of Marxist socialism is still palpable, we have some immunity to it. Regrettably, we have no such immunity to ESG, so-called stakeholder capitalism, and other modern proposals to dispossess investors and workers in the quest to force business to promote social objectives. Today, the siren song of "business should do more to promote the common good" seems new and appealing—dangerously so.

The Enlightenment was founded on the principle that people own the fruits of their own labor and thrift; ESG, stakeholder or accountable capitalism, and similar proposals that force workers and investors to share their economic rewards are instead a throwback to the medieval concept of communal property. While no law mandating ESG or accountable capitalism has ever passed, the battle to overturn the Enlightenment is now being fought in corporate boardrooms and investor meetings all across America.

According to Ernst & Young, nonmanagement-supported shareholder resolutions proposing new ESG goals exploded in 2022–23, rising by more than 70 percent versus 2021.[19] Though shareholders repeatedly defeat many such proposals, corporations often bow to political pressure and grant concessions in return for dropping the resolutions. Shareholder activism supported by index funds—in which firms vote other peoples' shares—has also won major concessions from companies like Exxon.

As resources have poured into index funds, the percentage of the overall stock market held passively has grown exponentially. Today more than one-third of all public equities in America are held in index funds or their equivalent. Index funds are now the largest shareholders of more than 40 percent of all US companies.[20] There is good reason for this: Index funds are cost-effective and efficient for end investors, ranking them among the most beneficial financial innovations in history. But problems arise when index fund managers engage in unauthorized and politicized corporate governance, voting shares that do not belong to them to promote objectives that do not serve the asset owners' long-run financial interests.

Since index fund managers are voting investor shares that they do not actually own, they have a built-in incentive to vote in ways that enhance their public image and asset-gathering strategies at the possible expense of the company whose shares are being voted. All actions of investment managers and their proxy advisers are nominally subject to fiduciary standards. Increasingly, those fiduciary standards are being flouted.

America developed the world's most successful economy by allowing private wealth to serve private interest, not some presumed, evolving, and ever-growing public interest. By politicizing corporate-governance and business decisions, ESG too often undermines private-sector efficiency. Aggressive ESG agendas can and have cheated investors, workers, and consumers all in the contrary name of promoting their supposed interest.

Almost all discussion of ESG, whether by advocates or opponents, has been premised on the assumption that, to the extent promoting ESG objectives reduces efficiency, raises prices, and reduces profits, only "rich" investors and corporations suffer any harm. Supporters of ESG regularly assert their efforts will enable investors to "do well and good" at the same time, claiming ESG policies somehow do not penalize profitability. Even if costs do go up, they assert, corporations should justifiably bear them because ESG is effectively promoting the public interest.

Opponents of ESG have rightly emphasized that there is no such thing as a "rich" corporation. Corporations are legal entities owned by shareowners—of whom there are a great many. As much as three-quarters of all equity investment in America is held by public and private pension funds, 401(k)s, individual retirement accounts, and insurance companies to support retirement, income annuities, and death benefits. Based on these data, to the extent ESG is extracting value from "rich" corporations, it is instead diminishing the financial security of millions of American retirees and workers.

But when ESG corporate provisions lower efficiency, raise costs, and reduce profitability, those costs do not fall exclusively on the investor.

Arguably, in its most idealistic form, Marxism dispossesses capital in an effort to benefit labor. In the real world, the result was always a destruction of the interests of capital and labor and ultimately prosperity and freedom—none of which were Marx's intended objectives. Similarly, ESG investing, aimed at forcing private business to promote public purposes, is an assault on not just capital but labor and the consumer as well. Forcing business to serve the interests of "stakeholders" lowers efficiency and raises prices, passing additional costs on to consumers.

Where this occurs, the first element of society to bear the cost of ESG-induced inefficiency is the American consumer. The costs that can't be passed on to the consumer because of competitive conditions in the market will be absorbed partly by the investor and partly by workers. Historically, labor and capital have shared rewards and costs in an approximate ratio of 70 percent to 30 percent.[21] To the extent that ESG drives up cost, the share of that burden not borne by consumers would be disproportionally borne by labor as compared to capital. As a result, ESG investments that increase a company's production costs represent an attack on workers' pension and wages.

The ESG debate's focus on the potential cost to capital has provided a shield for ESG proponents who have been able to fall back on the simple assertion that "rich" corporations can afford the cost and by implication are making too much money anyway. The real beneficiaries of ESG are those who get to determine which interests are subsidized. Those interests are largely benefited at the expense of the consumer, investor, and worker. When the full ramifications of ESG investing are understood, the resulting costs prove far harder to justify, especially in a public debate.

Fiduciary Rules Require Profit Maximization

The efforts of ESG proponents to force business to serve the financial interests of their chosen stakeholders—for example, by reducing greenhouse-gas emissions—runs afoul of the most fundamental requirement in corporate stewardship and investing: *fiduciary responsibility*. In corporate stewardship and investing, fiduciary rules and practices preclude giving priority to anything that dilutes shareowners' financial interests unless explicitly instructed to the contrary by the investor—and often not even then.

Fiduciary concepts are fundamental. The term itself derives from the Latin term *fiduciaries*, which means "entrusted" or "held in trust." John Locke first popularized the theory of "fiduciary government" in his famous 1689 treatises defending democratic rule. Locke maintained people have a right to resist any regime that betrays their trust. Trust is an essential element for the functioning of all markets and societies. Fiduciary rules have been put into place to preserve it.

In the US, the Investment Advisers Act of 1940 stipulates two basic fiduciary duties all investment advisers must provide their clients: the duty of *care* and the duty of *loyalty*. In short, investment advisers are required at all times to put their clients' financial interests ahead of all other concerns, especially their own. To the duties of care and loyalty, obedience, confidentiality, prudence, and disclosure are often added. In practice, this has meant advisers must always promote their clients' direct financial interests *unless explicitly instructed otherwise.* An example of this might be a client who requests a religious or ESG screen for their investments.

Even in these cases, however, the adviser is required to disclose to the investor how such constraints may negatively affect their costs, performance, or desired liquidity before implementation. This means that, even when clients request a religious or ESG screen, the adviser must endeavor to understand first why such a constraint is desired and, second, whether the underlying goals their clients seek can be achieved more effectively and efficiently in some other way. Were advisers not informing their clients that their goals might be met more cheaply or effectively, they would fail in their duty of care, loyalty, and giving financial priority to their client's interests.

In 1974, in response to the repeated abuses of pension funds by union leaderships, Congress passed ERISA, which provides an explicit definition of fiduciary duty. The fiduciary must act "solely in the interest of" and "for the exclusive purpose of providing benefits" to the investor.[22] In this respect, index funds that vote to enable stakeholders to override public company boards in support of many ESG issues violate their fiduciary duties. Similarly, government agencies that enforce stakeholder demands through their regulatory powers are also violating the same rules.

No discussion of fiduciary responsibilities for corporate directors would be complete without mentioning Milton Friedman's pivotal 1970 *New York Times* essay "The Social Responsibility of Business Is to Increase Its Profits." Friedman was motivated to write this essay because "discussions of the 'social responsibilities of business' are notable for their analytical looseness and lack of rigor."[23] Times have not changed: Analytical looseness and lack of rigor characterize all ESG techniques and definitions today. Friedman goes on to note that, in a free-enterprise, private-property system, all corporate executives are employees of the owners of their business, which of course are their shareowners. The desires of shareowners, Friedman memorably summarized, "generally will be to make as much money as possible while conforming to the basic rules of the society, both those embodied in law and those embodied in ethical custom."

Friedman does not mean to disparage charitable activities with this statement. In fact, he explicitly endorses multiple types of corporate entities that are established for eleemosynary purposes. After all, hospitals, nongovernmental organizations, and many educational institutions are corporations too. Instead, his point is that the vast majority of private businesses have not been formed to conduct charity; they instead engage in risky commercial endeavors with the ultimate goal of enriching their owners, legally and responsibly.

Where and how commercial risk is born has proved crucial to human flourishing. In short, history has shown that those who are knowingly risking their own capital—rather than someone else's—do so far more successfully. Much of economics can be reduced to two words: *Incentives matter*. Obviously, private business owners and individuals are also legally entitled and properly incentivized to invest their own money, bearing their successes and failures as market circumstances dictate.

In recent years, shareowner resolutions have increasingly focused on environmental and social concerns. While several of these resolutions have arguably been for the long-term benefit of shareowners, the bulk have favored nonfinancial ESG agendas that imperil long-term value creation. In 2021, 20 percent of the 170 environmental and social shareowner proposals voted on by S&P 500 companies received majority support. These included proposals to lower greenhouse-gas emissions and a range of diversity, equity, and social inclusion proposals. In 2022, only 12.5 percent of these same kinds of ESG proposals passed—but because there were 289 proposals, more were adopted (36 vs. 34).[24]

As of July 2023, the number of environmental and stakeholder proposals has continued to climb, but only seven out of 296 have passed. According to the stewardship teams at Vanguard and BlackRock, the declining quality of proposed ESG measures and their increasing lack of financial materiality reduced their support of ESG initiatives in 2023 versus 2021–22.[25] But perhaps a growing political backlash against ESG from conservative states, members of Congress, and investors also changed their risk-reward calculus.

In a further effort to mute criticism from conservative states, some fund managers have begun offering a small subset of their clients more stewardship voting rights options. For example, Black-Rock now permits a portion of its institutional and retail clients to choose from a menu of voting options ranging from the standard Institutional Shareholder Services and Glass Lewis paradigms to certain religious screen options and more aggressive sustainability agendas. Those who do not choose a voting paradigm default to the BlackRock standard option. Shareowners are also allowed to vote their own shares—though few should ever be expected to do so given hundreds of thousands of votes are taken every year across the widest index funds.

None of these options meet the index fund's fiduciary responsibility. The index fund should either vote the shares solely in the shareowner's economic interest or provide the shareowner an explanation of how ESG voting might affect returns and require the shareholder to declare their desire to have their shares voted to dilute their return and promote ESG goals. Stated differently, fiduciary responsibility requires that shareowners' financial interests always be given priority unless they verifiably opt in to a contrary regime. Without authorized consent, fiduciary standards require that financial interests must always prevail.

While the federal government has continued to fail to enforce fiduciary requirements, states have moved aggressively in dealing with the problem. Ten states have enacted legislation to strengthen state fiduciary laws. States have begun to withdraw state pension fund investments from funds that promote ESG objectives at the expense of investors.[26] It seems only a matter of time until the Supreme Court steps in and addresses the fiduciary issue.

ESG Does Neither Well nor Much Good

The hoped-for outcome and explicit promise of the UN's Principles for Responsible Investment were to unleash a wave of new capital commitments that promoted the attainment of the UN's Sustainable Development Goals while generating returns equal to or above the market—that is, "doing well while doing good." It was and remains a compelling idea. Who among us does not want to have our cake (i.e., make the world a better place) while eating it too (achieving great returns)? "Doing well while doing good" captures the imagination of many investors, especially younger generations. Making terrific returns while somehow simultaneously making the world more just and the environment more sustainable is an appealing dream.

A dream too good to be true, however. Hard evidence shows ESG funds have neither performed well nor generated the type of environmental and social benefits their supporters hoped for. As an asset class, the ESG public equity investment fund universe underperformed the broad market on average by more than 250 basis points annually in the five-year period ending in December 2022 (6.3 percent vs. 8.9 percent).[27] According to American financial services firm Morningstar, 2022 was the worst-performing calendar year for sustainable funds since it began tracking them. The year 2023 was no better.

But equally important, there is little evidence that ESG investing generated meaningful social or environmental gains since the UN's Principles for Responsible Investment were adopted—almost none that wouldn't have taken place without ESG, that is. Rather than doing well and doing good, ESG has done far too little of either.

The precise failures of ESG investing have manifested in three different dimensions: data, definitions, and process. Any one of these failures would normally turn an enthusiast into a skeptic. Taken together, they amount to a damning indictment of the entire ESG project.

Take ESG data, for example. According to research by Florian Berg, Julian Kolbel, and Roberto Rigobon of the Massachusetts Institute of Technology and the University of Zurich, ESG ratings among the top six rating agencies—KLD, Sustainalytics, Moody's, S&P, Refinitiv, and MSCI—correlate only 0.31–0.71 percent of the time, or a pitiful average of one time out of two.[28] Compare this with the 0.98 percent correlation for the three major credit rating agencies—Moody's, S&P, and Fitch—and you see how standardization of ESG rating methodologies remains a distant pipe dream. We are now 15 years into the ESG movement, yet there is no output conformity among ESG rating agencies. Jay Clayton, former chairman of the SEC, succinctly summarized why: ESG ratings are "over-inclusive."[29]

In short, ESG ratings fail because they are trying to measure too many variables at once. Attempting to put every ESG material risk found in Table 1 together in a single score is so complex and fraught that industry-wide concurrence on how best to do so is not and never will be possible. No one would forecast that the weather tomorrow will be AA or BBB, which is how MSCI scores ESG. Weather forecasts must include the temperature, chance for precipitation, and wind conditions to have any actionable meaning. Similarly, for ESG ratings to have any meaning, they must be disaggregated. Composite ESG scores, which are now used as industry standards, are largely meaningless.

The second challenge facing ESG defenders concerns definitions. As with data divergence, there is no single standard defining what an ESG or sustainable investment product actually is. For example, according to Bloomberg, there are $45 trillion worth of investment products in the marketplace that carry either an ESG or sustainable investment label.[30] These are products that end investors have chosen because they share some kind of sustainable or social purpose. But just like with divergent ESG ratings, it is genuinely impossible to know what these labels actually mean. Bloomberg's definitions of ESG are not shared by others.

The most advanced effort to establish a proper taxonomy for ESG investment products exists in Europe. The European Union's Sustainable Finance Disclosure Regulation now classifies funds as Article 6, 8, or 9 depending on their perceived levels of ESG sanctity and sustainability. Article 6 funds have no environmental or social objectives, Article 8 funds have some nonfinancial objectives, and Article 9 funds have explicit, determinative nonfinancial goals.

But even the EU keeps changing these definitions and conditions for classification, often dramatically. For example, after Vladimir Putin's brutal invasion of Ukraine, the European Commission readmitted natural gas and nuclear power as qualified, investable assets in Article 8 and 9 funds. (Note that natural gas and nuclear had previously been excluded.) This dramatic shift merits reflection. The ever-changing beliefs of a collection of bureaucrats are not exactly conducive to long-run investment planning, especially given that liquefied natural gas and nuclear power investments require long lead times. It is only fair to ask how sound an investment paradigm can be if it can change so dramatically from one day to the next.

Bloomberg, Morningstar, the SEC, and the EU's investment regulatory bodies have yet to agree on what is and is not a sustainable investment product. No one can say with certainty what will be designated as "sustainable" in the decades to come.

Which brings us to the third and perhaps most damning failure of ESG investing: *investment process*. The year 2022 may have been bad for ESG because of the chronic underweighting of oil and gas, but long-term underperformance is literally baked into every ESG product that is a small subset of a broad index. ESG investment funds violate the central insight for which economist Harry Markowitz earned a Nobel Prize in 1990.

Markowitz's award-winning research revealed optimal portfolios must comprise a broad mix of uncorrelated assets. Investments that are uncorrelated with one another lower the volatility risk of a portfolio while improving returns. Stated succinctly, Markowitz proved that, for any given measure of volatility risk, the more diversified a portfolio is, the more certain it is to generate higher returns. Beating the market is notoriously difficult because broad indexes like the S&P 500 and MSCI Global Index intentionally embrace broad industry and company diversification.[31]

As ESG indexes intentionally exclude whole industries, screening out as much as 80 percent of the entire market, it is all but certain they will continue to underperform broad indexes over time. This problem is compounded by the fact that ESG investing excludes sectors on political grounds rather than on any profit-maximizing strategy. Broad indexes like the S&P 500 are constantly updated in real time, with sector weights changing automatically as market capitalizations change.

No ESG index or fund yet matches the sophistication and inclusiveness of broad-market indexes, nor do they have any reasonable prospect of doing so. Moreover, widespread claims of "greenwashing" will continue as ESG funds and products attempt to better track broader indexes while still making some claim to be "sustainable." Why? Eliminating oil and gas exposure in an ESG fund introduces a form of "tracking error" or intentional divergence from broader indexes, almost invariably resulting in long-term financial underperformance that no fiduciary can long tolerate. ESG funds that fail to include any oil and gas for the foreseeable future will experience broad periods of underperformance such as occurred during 2022, igniting fiduciary criticisms. This said, any fund that includes oil and gas will be criticized for being insufficiently green. In this sense, versus broad index investments, ESG products are invariably structured to be lose-lose. They will fail in terms of either performance, exposure to presumably non-sustainable industries, or both.

ESG investing violates Markowitz's investment principles by focusing on overweighting sectors somehow deemed to be more virtuous—like technology—while underweighting sectors like oil and gas, which are seen as environmental scofflaws. Putin's invasion of Ukraine, the pandemic spending blowout, and overly expansive Fed policy sent inflation rates up dramatically, altering the cheap-energy, low-interest-rate environment. Portfolios with heavy over- and under-weightings were punished, validating Markowitz's theorem. Oil and gas stocks were the best-performing sectors of the market in 2022, while technology shares declined an average of 25 percent.[32] Any investor who put $10,000 into an average ESG fund in 2017 had only about $13,500 at the end of 2022, versus $15,250 had the investor stayed invested in the broader, non-ESG-screened market.

Doing More Good Often Requires Trade-Offs

Has ESG investing changed company behavior by penalizing non-ESG-compliant firms and rewarding those embracing ESG? All investments involve trade-offs. If avoiding a company's stock somehow made it into a "better" company and, in turn, the world a better place, ESG investing may have a normative leg to stand on. But according to significant research, divesting from a company does not fundamentally change its behavior.

A 2023 study by Davidson Heath and Matthew Ringgenberg of the University of Utah, Daniele Macciocchi of the University of Miami, and Roni Michaely of the University of Hong Kong found that socially responsible investment funds haven't changed individual firms' behaviors in any discernible manner. Their detailed study reviewed all socially responsible investment funds from 2010 to 2019, including the companies they invested in. They concluded, "We find no evidence that SRI [socially responsible investment] funds have any impact on corporate [environmental and social] conduct." In fact, their evidence found ESG investors would be more impactful if they did the exact opposite—invest rather than divest: "SRI funds could have a bigger impact if they invested in 'brown' firms [companies that do not meet ESG standards] and worked to improve their conduct."[33]

The findings of Professor Heath and his colleagues are consistent with other academic studies and decades of prior investment experience. For example, Professors Brad Cornell of the University of California, Los Angeles, and Aswath Damodaran of New York University investigated the economic performance of companies with high ESG ratings. They concluded, "Telling firms that being socially responsible will deliver higher growth, profits and value is false advertising."[34]

Socially responsible investing based on exclusion does not make industries more socially responsible. The ineffectiveness of ESG funds to promote more virtuous behavior is merely the latest example of the impotence of divestment as a corporate engagement strategy. Indeed, dating back to the abhorrent days of slave trading, the history of socially responsible investing has proved impotent relative to its intended effects. Slave trading persisted for centuries even though more than three-quarters of the world's capital refused to participate in it, simply because one-quarter still did. Moreover, such investors received a premium return for doing so.

Similarly, many religiously inspired investors have for decades avoided the shares of four so-called "sin industries"—alcohol, firearms, gambling, and tobacco. Can we not see how much impact billions of dollars of divestments have had on drinking, smoking, gambling, and illegal firearm use? Literally *none*.

Attempting to change the use of certain products and practices by trying to alter the funding of those ventures is a failed strategy. If you want to lower consumption of cigarettes or petroleum products, for example, you must focus on consumer demand, not supply. Meanwhile, market forces work to offset the impact of virtue investing as higher returns on shunned industries attract other investors' capital. Institutions that divested capital from Philip Morris's stock because they abhor cigarettes never stopped one person from smoking; other investors were always willing to take their place, and those investors' returns were higher. Consider again the findings of Cornell and Damadoran: "Evidence that socially responsible firms have lower discount rates, and thereby investors have lower expected returns, is stronger than the evidence that socially responsible firms deliver higher profits or growth."[35]

Attempting to do good more often than not means doing less well. Whenever an enterprise is legal and profitable, capital will flow to it. That ESG-driven divestiture would somehow produce different results than socially responsible investing belies centuries of experience and simple logic. Moreover, the ability to influence corporate behaviors through active share ownership, proxy voting, and board elections is forgone through divestiture. Divestiture leaves corporate governance in the hands of those more inclined to allow corporate practices to proceed unimpeded.

But there is also another unintended consequence worth mentioning. If ESG investing actually changed company behavior from maximizing profits to promoting ESG goals, that company would be less efficient, with higher costs and lower profits. In time, it would attract less capital from market-driven investors than a similar company not dominated by ESG. The impact of ESG investment on the company deemed to be virtuous would therefore be at least partially offset by a decline in non-ESG investing in that company over time.

ESG investing has proved disappointing in both spheres of influence at which it pledged to excel. It has neither generated market investment returns nor unleashed a wave of new investments that have effectively promoted the UN's Sustainable Development Goals. With more than $120 trillion of assets under the direct control of the UN Principles for Responsible Investment signatories, a growing number of investors are asking themselves whether there is a better way forward. Happily for them and those who seek double-bottom-line returns, there is. The alternative is called "impact investing," in which measurable and verifiable economic, social, and environmental benefits are generated along with financial returns.

Table 2 shows a helpful way to think about the types of trade-offs that will be necessary as one considers multiple objectives beyond financial returns for one's investments. On the far left of this continuum are all traditional investments, in which financial returns are paramount and investors are unwilling to sacrifice their returns for other objectives. All asset classes are relevant in this "financial first" investment world, including public and private credit, venture capital, private equity, stock investments, fixed income, real assets, and even cash.

Moving to the right of the continuum, investors must be willing to forgo some income to achieve their nonpecuniary goals. This includes socially responsible investing, forms of sustainable investments, and select ESG thematic funds.

On the far right, purely philanthropic investment takes place. This includes charitable grants and donations. Note, however, that these gifts can also be made as investments, in noncash form. Forgivable loans, social impact bonds, and even intangibles like time and advice can be and often are the difference between a failed nonprofit and a highly impactful nonprofit getting off the ground and thriving. In the impact-investment world, moreover, purely concessionary startup capital increasingly morphs over time into economic investments that attract successful second- and third-stage financings.

For most individual investors who want to do well and do good, the best option remains to invest money to do well and then use superior returns to do good. In practice, this requires long-term exposures to broad investment indexes, not ESG-screened ones.

Of course, it is also important to remember that doing well in and of itself does a lot of good. When investors use their capital to maximize returns, they do so by attempting to invest in things that put their capital to the best use, in the process increasing productivity, wages, and growth. Efficient investing does tangible good for mankind by doing well. A brief look at Figures 1 and 2 makes this point better than any words could.

Humankind didn't dramatically lower poverty or increase global per capita income beyond any level that would have been imaginable at the end of World War II by investing to do good. Rather, the great mass of mankind escaped poverty and achieved prosperity as a result of profit-focused, market-driven investments. As Friedman observed, when businesses maximize profits within the rule of law, society benefits, not least because poverty is diminished.

Contributing the fruits of investment success allows the giver to target their gift in areas where they can see a direct impact. For example, Henry Ford obsessed about making his cars so cheap that every worker who built them could afford one. He was so successful at this singular economic objective that he put the world on wheels, enriched multiple communities, built the world's then-largest fortune, and ended up giving most of his wealth away.

The distinction between ESG and impact investment comes down to two fundamental elements. First, all impact investments must exhibit verified additionality, in which incremental environmental or social improvements can be tangibly measured and directly attributed to the investment that has been made. Second, while not always the case, on average, impact investing will be marginally concessionary in nature. Providing potable water in remote parts of Africa or microfinancing to small businesses in South America may not change the world or generate massive returns,

Table 2. Positioning Investments on the "Do Well–Do

Traditional Investing	Impact Investing		
Financial First	Mission-Related Investments		
Market Rate	Market Rate		
• Seeks to maximize risk-adjusted rates of return • Selection driven by traditional investment characteristics	• Seeks both financial and social returns on investments • Targets a risk-adjusted market rate of return while supporting the investor's mission by generating a positive social or environmental impact		
	Socially Responsible Investing (Negative Screening)	Sustainable (ESG)	Thematic (Impact)
	• Values-based • Excludes investments to align with investor's values	• Positive tilting • Considers ESG factors' criteria when investing	• Investing in solution-oriented companies • Focuses on specific themes

- Equity
- Fixed income
- Cash
- Alternative investments
- Certificates of deposit
- Mutual funds, exchange-traded funds, and unit investment trusts
- Separate accounts
- Private partnerships

Source: Sorenson Impact Foundation.

Good" Continuum

Impact Investing		Traditional Philanthropy
Impact First	**Program-Related Investments**	**Charitable Grants**
Blended	**Concessionary**	**Donations**

• Investments intended to prioritize measurable social and environmental impact over a financial return
 	
• Investors may accept below-market (concessionary) returns
	• Investments defined by the IRS tax code whose:
	
	  • Primary purpose is to accomplish one or more exempt purposes
	
	  • Production of income or appreciation of property is not a significant purpose
	
	• Investors may accept below-market (concessionary) returns
	
	• Eligible to count toward annual IRS-required minimum spending
		• No expectation of any financial return
		
		• Aligned with values or mission
		
		• Typically counts toward minimum IRS spending requirement

	• Equity • Loans and loan guarantees • Social impact bonds • Private partnerships • Cash • Securities • Other proprietary • Intangibles	

but they fundamentally change the world of those who get clean water and financing to invest in their dreams. Though they may generate a lower rate of return than other for-profit strategies, this forgone income was understood in advance and a price the asset owner willingly and intentionally elected to pay.

The world of impact investing is quickly evolving. It offers a growing array of genuine "do well, do good" opportunities for asset owners. In the decades ahead, we will speak of impact investing the same way we speak of private equity and venture capital today.

The Future of ESG

In 2023, then–Vanguard CEO Tim Buckley shocked the investment community by withdrawing his firm from the $59 trillion Net Zero Asset Managers initiative. At the same time, he announced, "Our research indicates that ESG investing does not have any advantage over broad-based investing."[36] Given that ESG funds receive higher fees than broad-based funds, his actions were a powerful signal. As the public comes to understand the failure of ESG investing to achieve its stated goals and increasingly demands that fiduciary duty be respected by those who are entrusted with the life savings of American investors, ESG investing will be increasingly challenged legally and practically.

Of course, some ideas die more slowly than they should. If ESG lives on, it would not be the first time in history that an idea overstayed its potential utility. Consider the life of one of the Enlightenment's main contributors, Sir Isaac Newton. While his 1687 work *Principia Mathematica* summarized all mathematical knowledge in his day, more than one-third of his recorded works dealt with fanciful alchemical experiments. One of history's greatest geniuses obsessed over the possible creation of gold from base materials and the discovery of "the philosopher's stone," an element that was presumed to grant its human possessor the possibility of eternal life.

Just as we now know alchemy was always misguided—gold is an element, unique unto itself—ESG is a wrongly conceived paradigm. However noble its intents may have been, it has been wrongly designed and executed. ESG does less well and good than a combination of investing for profit and using the profits for philanthropy and impact investing. The sooner investors, regulators, the asset-management industry, and other financial intermediaries realize this, the better off the world will be.

The basic appeal of ESG is and has always been its proponents' ability to promote their vision of how to do good with someone else's money. However noble their intents may have been, those proponents are in fact doing more harm than good.

The chapters in this book make many of the points we have tried to summarize here, but in greater detail. In them you will find deeper discussions about fiduciary standards, the inefficiencies of ESG investing, flawed ESG rating methodologies, and the historic analogy between pre-Enlightenment times and ESG's mistaken attempt to enrich society by extracting rents from workers, consumers, and capital owners. They also show how impact investing is a viable alternative for those who genuinely want their capital to *do well and do good*.

ESG, at its root, is a return to the pre-Enlightenment world where a self-chosen elite use nondemocratic means to extract the rewards that come from the sweat of the workers' brows and the sacrifice of their thrift. We have seen this drama play out many times before. The sooner we end the ESG experiment, the sooner we can restore the principles that have always allowed humanity to flourish.

Notes

1. G.A. Res. 217 (III) A, Universal Declaration of Human Rights (Dec. 10, 1948).

2. World Trade Organization, "Evolution of Trade Under the WTO: Handy Statistics," https://www.wto.org/english/res_e/statis_e/trade_evolution_e/evolution_trade_wto_e.htm.

3. UN Principles for Responsible Investment, "Quarterly Signatory Update," https://www.unpri.org/signatories/signatory-resources/quarterly-signatory-update.

4. UN Principles for Responsible Investment, "A Blueprint for Responsible Investment," YouTube, August 21, 2017, https://www.unpri.org/about-us/a-blueprint-for-responsible-investment.

5. Terrence Keeley, *Sustainable: Moving Beyond ESG to Impact Investing* (New York: Columbia University Press, 2022).

6. S.B. 253, 2023 Leg. (Cal 2023); and European Commission, "Corporate Sustainability Reporting," https://finance.ec.europa.eu/capital-markets-union-and-financial-markets/company-reporting-and-auditing/company-reporting/corporate-sustainability-reporting_en.

7. US Department of Labor, "Fiduciary Responsibilities," https://www.dol.gov/general/topic/retirement/fiduciaryresp.

8. Elizabeth Warren, "Accountable Capitalism Act," 2018, https://www.warren.senate.gov/imo/media/doc/Accountable%20Capitalism%20Act%20One-Pager.pdf; and Accountable Capitalism Act, S. 3348, 115th Cong., 2nd sess. (2018).

9. Kylie MacLellan, "UK's Labour Plans to Make Companies Give Shares to Workers," Reuters, September 24, 2018, https://www.reuters.com/article/us-britain-politics-labour-mcdonnell-idUSKCN1M401C.

10. Chuck Schumer and Bernie Sanders, "Schumer and Sanders: Limit Corporate Stock Buybacks," *New York Times*, February 3, 2019, https://www.nytimes.com/2019/02/03/opinion/chuck-schumer-bernie-sanders.html.

11. Gregory Clark, "The Condition of the Working Class in England, 1209–2004," *Journal of Political Economy* 113, no. 6 (December 2005):

1307–40, https://www.jstor.org/stable/10.1086/498123.

12. Adam Smith, "Chapter X: On Wages and Profit in the Different Employments of Labour and Stock," Marxists Internet Archive, https://www.marxists.org/reference/archive/smith-adam/works/wealth-of-nations/book01/ch10b.htm.

13. Clark, "The Condition of the Working Class in England, 1209–2004."

14. N. F. R. Crafts, "Economic Growth in France and Britain, 1830–1910: A Review of the Evidence," *Journal of Economic History* 44, no. 1 (March 1984): Table 1, 51, https://www.jstor.org/stable/2120555.

15. UK Office of National Statistics, "How Has Life Expectancy Changed over Time?," September 9, 2015, https://www.ons.gov.uk/peoplepopulationandcommunity/birthsdeathsandmarriages/lifeexpectancies/articles/howhaslifeexpectancychangedovertime/2015-09-09.

16. Thomas E. Jordan, "An Index of the Quality of Life for Victorian Children and Youth, the VICY Index," *Social Indicators Research* 27, no. 3 (November 1992): 257–77, https://www.jstor.org/stable/27520959.

17. Phil Gramm and Amity Shlaes, "The 'Gilded Age' Myth, Then and Now," *Wall Street Journal*, May 7, 2023, https://www.wsj.com/articles/the-gilded-age-myth-then-and-now-income-inequality-progressive-movement-economic-output-507dbc69.

18. Karl Marx, "Manifesto of the Communist Party," in *Great Books of the Western World*, ed. Robert Maynard Hutchins (Encyclopedia Britannica, 1952), 50:421.

19. Jamie Smith and David A. Hunker, "What Directors Need to Know About the 2023 Proxy Season," Ernst & Young, July 19, 2023, https://www.ey.com/en_us/board-matters/what-directors-need-to-know-about-the-2023-proxy-season.

20. Keeley, *Sustainable*.

21. William C. Randolph, "International Burdens of the Corporate Income Tax" (working paper, Congressional Budget Office, Washington, DC, August 2006), https://www.cbo.gov/sites/default/files/109th-congress-2005-2006/workingpaper/2006-09_0.pdf.

22. US Department of Labor, "Fiduciary Responsibilities."

23. Milton Friedman, "The Social Responsibility of Business Is to Increase Its Profits," *New York Times*, September 13, 1970, https://www.nytimes.com/1970/09/13/archives/a-friedman-doctrine-the-social-responsibility-of-business-is-to.html.

24. Smith and Hunker, "What Directors Need to Know About the 2023 Proxy Season."

25. BlackRock, *Investment Stewardship Annual Report: January 1– December 31, 2022*, 2023, https://www.blackrock.com/corporate/literature/publication/annual-stewardship-report-2022.pdf; and BlackRock, *2023 Global Voting Spotlight: Advancing Our Clients' Financial Interests*, 2023, https://www.blackrock.com/corporate/literature/publication/2023-investment-stewardship-voting-spotlight.pdf.

26. Andy Puzder, "Red States Have Slowed the ESG Juggernaut," *Wall Street Journal*, June 14, 2023, https://www.wsj.com/articles/red-states-have-slowed-the-esg-juggernaut-environmental-social-governance-shareholders-investing-7308cb8d.

27. Terrence Keeley, "ESG Does Neither Much Good nor Very Well," *Wall Street Journal*, September 12, 2022, https://www.wsj.com/articles/esg-does-neither-much-good-nor-very-well-evidence-composite-scores-impact-reports-strategy-jay-clayton-rating-agents-11663006833.

28. Florian Berg, Julian Kolbel, and Roberto Rigobon, "Aggregate Confusion: The Divergence of ESG Ratings," *Review of Finance* 26, no. 6 (November 2022): 1315–44, https://academic.oup.com/rof/article/26/6/1315/6590670. In a more extreme case, the CFA Institute found that correlations between two environmental, social, and governance (ESG) rating providers—Institutional Shareholder Services and S&P—were only 0.14 percent. When rating systems align only one time out of seven, neither can be trusted.

29. Declan Harty, "SEC's Clayton Expresses Skepticism over ESG Ratings," *S&P Global*, May 28, 2020, https://www.spglobal.com/marketintelligence/en/news-insights/latest-news-headlines/sec-s-clayton-expresses-skepticism-over-esg-ratings-58828014.

30. Bloomberg, "ESG May Surpass $41 Trillion Assets in 2022, but Not Without Challenges, Finds Bloomberg Intelligence," press release,

January 24, 2022, https://www.bloomberg.com/company/press/esg-may-surpass-41-trillion-assets-in-2022-but-not-without-challenges-finds-bloomberg-intelligence.

31. This is not to demean the occasional investment outperformer, like Warren Buffett. But the average investor is not Buffett. Instead, individuals with more modest savings and less sophistication must choose an index to buy and hold over long periods of time for efficiency and performance reasons. Because of their detailed methods of updating and evolution, only one institutional investor in seven outperforms the S&P 500 over any five-year period, and only one in 10 outperforms it over any 10-year period. While Buffett is one of these few, even he has suffered long periods of index underperformance. It is also worth remembering the famous bet Buffett made in 2008 against the hedge fund industry. He bet $1 million that any professionally handpicked portfolio would underperform the S&P 500 over the ensuing decade—and won. Over the betting period, the hedge fund portfolio manager returned a mere 22 percent, while the S&P index fund registered a total 85.4 percent return. Beating the market is all but impossible for small investors. Screening bad ESG stocks out of broader indexes is a fool's errand. Given broad index efficiencies, it is impossible to imagine how ESG-driven divestment strategies will generate consistently superior returns in the future.

32. Ron Bousso, "Big Oil Doubles Profits in Blockbuster 2022," Reuters, February 8, 2023, https://www.reuters.com/business/energy/big-oil-doubles-profits-blockbuster-2022-2023-02-08.

33. Davidson Heath et al., "Does Socially Responsible Investing Change Firm Behavior?," *Review of Finance*, European Corporate Governance Institute, and University of Miami Business School, January 18, 2023, https://papers.ssrn.com/sol3/papers.cfm?abstract_id=3837706. Note that by "brown firms," the authors mean firms that are not aligned with the goals to hit net-zero emissions by 2050, outlined in the Paris agreement.

34. Bradford Cornell and Aswath Damadoran, "Valuing ESG: Doing Good or Sounding Good?," New York University, Stern School of Business, March 20, 2020, https://papers.ssrn.com/sol3/papers.cfm?abstract_id=3557432.

35. Cornell and Damadoran, "Valuing ESG."

36. Terrence Keeley, "Vanguard's CEO Bucks the ESG Orthodoxy," *Wall Street Journal*, February 26, 2023, https://www.wsj.com/articles/vanguards-ceo-bucks-the-esg-orthodoxy-tim-buckley-net-zero-emissions-united-nations-initiative-nzam-f6ae910d.

Keep Politics Out of the Boardroom

Phil Gramm and Mike Solon

Wall Street Journal, July 18, 2018[1]

Even in democratic governments constrained by constitutional limits, the interests of the governed and the governors don't align well. Government is inefficient by its very nature, spending other people's money and subject to the leeching effects of special interests. Corporate governance, in contrast, historically has been conducted by people spending their own money, subject to the will of shareholders with a common ownership interest in the company. Calvin Coolidge famously noted that "the chief business of the American people is business," because Americans are "profoundly concerned with producing, buying, selling, investing and prospering in the world."[2]

But today government is working to remake the dynamic business sector in its own feeble image. Reforms to enhance shareholder rights made it easier for small shareholders to initiate votes, but the new rules mostly have helped interest groups with nominal stock ownership promote their political objectives at shareholders' expense.

The rise of index funds, which own an ever-greater portion of US stocks, raises the specter of a vast number of shares being voted by fund managers and their proxy advisers who don't own the shares and may have a conflict of interest with the people who do. The Sarbanes-Oxley Act increased the proportion of independent directors on the boards of public companies, diluting the share of the board with a vested stake in good performance.

Today investors with a political agenda force major energy companies and banks to evaluate the impact of fossil fuel bans, though no government has ever instituted such a ban. A Manhattan Institute study estimates that 56 percent of proxy resolutions in Fortune 250 companies in 2017 dealt with social and environmental issues.[3] Even when shareholder votes repeatedly crush such proposals, the business operations of targeted companies suffer. And corporations sometimes bow to political pressure by granting concessions in return for dropping the resolutions.

The claim that investors can do good and well at the same time by investing in socially desirable objectives is reminiscent of Bill Clinton's 1992 campaign proposal to invest private pension funds in chosen public projects. When even union pension funds refused to put members' retirement at risk by making "publicly beneficial investments," President Clinton opted in 1995 to use the muscle of housing and bank regulators. Federal agencies pressured private financial institutions and Fannie Mae and Freddie Mac to promote affordable housing with subprime loans. The outcome of this experiment in promoting the public interest with private money is now called the financial crisis.

Arguments for imposing political and social objectives on business often are little more than rationalizations for forcing businesses to abide by values that have been rejected in Congress and the courts. Activists increasingly attempt to disguise their values with the cloak of fiduciary responsibility.

The rise of passive investing presents a similar challenge to good governance. With the cost advantage that comes from investing based on formulas, resources have gushed into index funds, which today total at least 25 percent of all equity investment in America. Index funds are now the largest shareholders of at least 40 percent of all public US companies.[4] When an index fund participates in corporate governance, conflicts of interest can arise.

Since funds are voting their investors' shares and not their own, they may be inclined to vote in a way that prioritizes their public image and fundraising above the performance of the company on which they're voting. When BlackRock, Vanguard, or State Street supports political resolutions, are they acting in the interest of their investors or themselves?

Court rulings and regulatory actions have undermined the requirements of fiduciary responsibility, which once protected investors against conflicts of interest. To restore those protections, the Securities and Exchange Commission (SEC) should reverse the guidance it offered in its 2004 Egan-Jones letter and its subsequent ruling on behalf of Institutional Shareholder Services, which allows investment managers to use proxy advisers to escape responsibility for conflicts of interest. The SEC and Labor Department should revise their 1988 "Avon" letters to remove the mandate that investment managers must vote their fund's proxies.

All actions of investment managers and proxy advisers should be subject to fiduciary standards, and activists should be held to the same liability standard as everyone else for false and misleading statements. The SEC should raise the ownership requirement for offering resolutions not directly related to the firm's profitability and set a higher threshold for reoffering resolutions that previously have been rejected.

In restoring fiduciary responsibility, the SEC should follow a recent Labor Department bulletin clarifying that "fiduciaries may not increase expenses, sacrifice investment returns, or reduce the security of plan benefits in order to promote collateral goals."[5] Congress also should codify these changes, starting with Rep. Sean Duffy's (R-WI) Corporate Governance Reform and Transparency Act, which the House passed in December 2017.

America created the world's most successful economy by allowing private wealth to serve private economic objectives rather than political ones. The politicization of business decisions threatens to bring the massive inefficiencies of government into the private sector, cheating investors, workers, and consumers in the process.

We are all free to invest our own money to promote broadly defined objectives. But when fund managers and investment advisers cast votes with shares owned by investors, the investors' interests must govern, rather than the interests of activists, managers, or advisers. We became the richest, freest, and happiest people on earth by letting American business focus on business. Political issues should be debated in Congress and state houses, not corporate boardrooms and shareholder meetings.

Notes

1. Phil Gramm and Mike Solon, "Keep Politics Out of the Boardroom," *Wall Street Journal*, July 18, 2018, https://www.wsj.com/articles/keep-politics-out-of-the-boardroom-1531952912.

2. Robert Sobel, "Essays, Papers & Addresses: Coolidge and American Business," Calvin Coolidge Presidential Foundation, 1988, https://coolidgefoundation.org/resources/essays-papers-addresses-35.

3. James R. Copland and Margaret M. O'Keefe, "Proxy Monitor 2017: Season Review," Manhattan Institute, Fall 2017, https://www.proxymonitor.org/Forms/pmr_15.aspx.

4. Claire Donnelly and Meghna Chakrabarti, "Are Index Funds Getting Too Powerful?," WBUR, August 7, 2023, https://www.wbur.org/onpoint/2023/08/07/how-index-funds-are-shaping-corporations-and-the-american-economy; and Jan Fichtner, Eelke M. Heemskerk, and Javier Garcia-Bernardo, "Hidden Power of the Big Three? Passive Index Funds, Re-Concentration of Corporate Ownership, and New Financial Risk," *Business and Politics* 19, no. 2 (June 2017): 298–326, https://www.cambridge.org/core/journals/business-and-politics/article/hidden-power-of-the-big-three-passive-index-funds-reconcentration-of-corporate-ownership-and-new-financial-risk/30AD689509AAD62F5B677E916C28C4B6.

5. US Department of Labor, Employee Benefits Security Administration, "Field Assistance Bulletin No. 2018-01—Superseded by 85 FR 72846 and 85 FR 81658," April 23, 2018, https://www.dol.gov/agencies/ebsa/employers-and-advisers/guidance/field-assistance-bulletins/2018-01.

Enemies of the Economic Enlightenment

Phil Gramm and Mike Solon

Wall Street Journal, April 15, 2019[1]

The 18th-century Enlightenment liberated mind, soul, and property, empowering people to think their own thoughts, worship their own gods, and benefit from the fruits of their own labor and thrift. As labor and capital came to serve their owners, not the crown, guild, church, or village, economies began to awaken from a thousand years of stagnation. The British Parliament stripped away the leaching influence of royal charters and initiated reforms that ultimately allowed businesses to incorporate simply by meeting preset capital requirements. Parliament further established that its laws would govern business—laws created in a process of open deliberation, not by the corrosive influences and rampant cronyism that were pervasive in the medieval marketplace.

Enlightenment philosophers recognized that the crown, guild, church, and village sometimes acted as rent seekers stripping away the rewards for work, thrift, and innovation and in the process inhibiting productive effort and progress. The Enlightenment established the principle that labor and capital are private property and not communal assets subject to involuntary sharing and thus unleashed the explosion of knowledge and production that drives human flourishing to this day.

Extraordinarily in America, the crown jewel and greatest beneficiary of the Enlightenment, political movements are afoot that seek to overturn the individual economic rights secured in the Enlightenment and return to a medieval world of subjects and subjugation.

Sen. Elizabeth Warren's (D-MA) Accountable Capitalism Act would harness large American corporations by imposing new federal charters under which businesses would swear medieval fealty to "stakeholders": "the general public," "the workforce," "the community," "the environment," and "societal factors." Sen. Warren would also mandate that employees elect 40 percent of board members at very large corporations. In most cases these stakeholders would not have to "stake" any of their toil or treasure, but, as they did in the Dark Ages, they would claim communal rights to share the fruits that flow from the sweat of the worker's brows, the saver's thrift, and the investor's venture.

As if to announce step two of the plan, the British Labour Party has now surpassed board-seat meddling and proposes giving employees a 10 percent ownership stake in major British corporations. And back in the US, Sens. Chuck Schumer (D-NY) and Bernie Sanders want to block corporate stock buybacks and possibly halt dividend payments to investors—including retirement funds—unless companies pay additional benefits to workers as well.

Whereas the Enlightenment was based on the principle that people own the fruits of their labor and thrift, "accountable capitalism" and similar proposals to force the sharing of economic rewards return the economy to the medieval concept of communal property. That system allows the powerful few to extort part of the fruits of your labor and capital because, as President Barack Obama would say, if you own a business, "you didn't build that."

While this debate will play out in elections over the next decade, a more imminent threat to the Enlightenment's economic legacy comes from the surreptitious battle being waged in shareholder meetings and corporate boardrooms across America. Political activists are pressuring companies to adopt political, social, and environmental policies that would subvert earnings that rightly belong to labor and capital.

Past attempts by courts and the Securities and Exchange Commission (SEC) to enhance shareholder rights have unintentionally empowered special-interest groups to subvert corporate governance, forcing corporations to deal with political and social problems they were never designed or empowered to tackle. The explosion of index funds, whose managers vote shares they do not own, has dramatically increased the danger political activists pose to sound governance and, in turn, to American prosperity.

Passive funds now manage more than 25 percent of US stock. Taken together, the three biggest funds constitute the largest shareholder in at least 40 percent of public US companies.[2] Their continued growth seems guaranteed, as they gain a tremendous price advantage by simply buying slices of various equity indexes rather than incurring the cost of analyzing each investment.

But such efficiency has a price. An index fund's profitability is not significantly affected by the performance of any given company in the index, since its competitors sell the same indexes. Therefore, index funds and their proxy advisers often have neither the in-depth knowledge nor the aligned interests to make judgments on specific questions that arise in the shareholder meetings of the companies in which they hold an ever-greater share of voting power.

When index funds vote their investors' shares on broad social and political issues, the problem is not only the lack of aligned interests and knowledge but that index funds often face glaring conflicts of interest. With high-profile social and political issues, the profitability of the scale-driven index fund business can be affected by how the public perceives their "social values" and how that affects the fund's marketing. That means the index fund's financial interest in each vote may often conflict with that of its investors.

Jack Bogle, the father of the index fund, urged legislation to impose a fiduciary duty on funds "to vote solely in the interest of the funds' shareholders."[3] But even enhanced fiduciary responsibility can't eliminate index funds' incentive to treat their marketing interests as a strong factor in the shareholder votes they cast.

On those issues, maybe it is time for the SEC to require index funds to poll their investors and vote their shares only as specifically directed. Without such limits, the economic interests of swelling index funds could convert "private purpose" C corporations into "public benefit" B corporations, and in the process overturn the economic Enlightenment.

History teaches that if we want to be prosperous and free, within the rule of law, we must let private interests create wealth and reap the rewards. Only after wealth has been created should we debate the costs and benefits of redistributing it to our desired social ends.

Notes

1. Phil Gramm and Mike Solon, "Enemies of the Economic Enlightenment," *Wall Street Journal*, April 15, 2019, https://www.wsj.com/articles/enemies-of-the-economic-enlightenment-11555366746. This article was adapted from Phil Gramm's testimony before the Banking Committee on April 2, 2019.

2. Claire Donnelly and Meghna Chakrabarti, "Are Index Funds Getting Too Powerful?," WBUR, August 7, 2023, https://www.wbur.org/onpoint/2023/08/07/how-index-funds-are-shaping-corporations-and-the-american-economy; and Jan Fichtner, Eelke M. Heemskerk, and Javier Garcia-Bernardo, "Hidden Power of the Big Three? Passive Index Funds, Re-Concentration of Corporate Ownership, and New Financial Risk," *Business and Politics* 19, no. 2 (June 2017): 298–326, https://www.cambridge.org/core/journals/business-and-politics/article/hidden-power-of-the-big-three-passive-index-funds-reconcentration-of-corporate-ownership-and-new-financial-risk/30AD689509AAD62F5B677E916C28C4B6.

3. John C. Bogle, "Bogle Sounds a Warning on Index Funds," *Wall Street Journal*, November 29, 2018, https://www.wsj.com/articles/bogle-sounds-a-warning-on-index-funds-1543504551.

Warren's Assault on Retiree Wealth

Phil Gramm and Mike Solon

Wall Street Journal, September 10, 2019[1]

Who owns the vast wealth of America? Old folks. According to the Federal Reserve, households headed by people over age 55 own 80 percent of the value of domestically owned stocks and the same share of America's total wealth.[2] Households headed by those ages 65 to 74 have an average of $1,066,000 in net worth, while those between ages 35 and 44 have less than a third as much on average, at $288,700.[3]

A socialist might see injustice in that inequality. But seniors know this wealth gap is the difference between the start and the finish of a career of work and thrift, making the last mortgage and retirement payments rather than the first. Seventy-two percent of the value of all domestically held stocks is owned by pension plans, 401(k)s, and individual retirement accounts (IRAs) or held by life insurance companies to fund annuities and death benefits. This wealth accumulated over a lifetime and benefits all Americans.

That means it's your life savings on the line—not the bankroll of some modern-day John D. Rockefeller—when Democrats push to limit companies' methods of enriching their shareholders. Several Democratic congressmen and presidential candidates have proposed to limit stock buybacks, which are estimated to have increased stock values by almost a fifth since 2011, as well as to block dividend payments, impose a new federal property tax, and tax the inside buildup of investments. Yet among all the

Democratic taxers and takers, no one would hit retirees harder than Sen. Elizabeth Warren (D-MA).

Her Accountable Capitalism Act would wipe out the single greatest legal protection retirees currently enjoy—the requirement that corporate executives and fund managers act as fiduciaries on investors' behalf. To prevent union bosses, money managers, or politicians from raiding pension funds, the 1974 Employee Retirement Income Security Act requires that a fiduciary shall manage a plan "solely in the interest of the participants and beneficiaries . . . for the exclusive purpose of providing benefits to participants and their beneficiaries."[4] The Securities and Exchange Commission imposes similar requirements on investment advisers, and state laws impose fiduciary responsibility on state-chartered corporations.

Sen. Warren would blow up these fiduciary-duty protections by rewriting the charter for every corporation with gross receipts of more than $1 billion. Every corporation, proprietorship, partnership, and limited-liability company of that size would be forced to enroll as a federal corporation under a new set of rules. Under this new Warren charter, companies currently dedicated to their shareholders' interest would be reordered to serve the interests of numerous new "stakeholders," including "the workforce," "the community," "customers," "the local and global environment," and "community and societal factors."

Eliminating corporations' duty to serve investors exclusively and forcing them to serve political interests would represent the greatest government taking in American history. Sen. Warren's so-called accountable capitalism raids the return that wealth provides to its owners, the vast majority of whom are present or near retirees. This subversion of capitalism would hijack Americans' wealth to serve many new masters who, unlike shareholders, don't have their life savings at stake in the companies that are collectivized.

After dividing retirees' rightful earnings eight ways to serve the politically favored, the Warren charter goes on to require that "not less than 2/5 of the directors of a United States corporation shall be elected by the employees."[5] With a mandate to share profits with seven other interest groups and 40 percent of the board chosen by non-investors, does anybody doubt that investors' wealth would be quickly devoured?

At best, every US company with gross revenues over $1 billion would be suddenly coerced into operating like a not-for-profit. But unlike legally recognized benefit corporations, the companies would be redirected to multiple competing purposes. A new Office of US Corporations would decide—and lawyers would sue to determine—whether those interests are satisfied, and only then would retirees receive the remaining crumbs. Only in Sen. Warren's socialist heaven would workers continue to sweat and sacrifice while their rewards go to publicly favored groups.

It is the fiduciary responsibility of every investment adviser, pension fund, 401(k), IRA, and life insurance company to tell its clients what would happen to their investments under Sen. Warren's bill. Her plan would devastate the income-generating capacity of every major company in America and decimate their market value in the process.

If the bill were passed, retirement plans and investors could attempt to sell their stocks and find new investments where their money would still work for them. They could sell their shares in the large companies subject to Sen. Warren's dispossession and buy into smaller companies with receipts below the $1 billion threshold, or they could look for investments abroad.

The problem is that everybody else would be trying to do the same. Investments built over a lifetime would be sold in a fire sale, with limited alternatives purchased in panic buying. While no econometric model could give a reliable estimate of the wealth destruction, no knowledgeable observer could doubt that an economic cataclysm would follow such a policy. "Accountable capitalism" would hit present and near retirees first and hardest, followed by American workers and the rest of the economy.

Sen. Warren would roll back the economic Enlightenment that gave us private property and economic freedom and plunge us back into the communal world of the Dark Ages. Like the village, guild, church, and crown of yore, government-empowered special interests would once again be allowed to extort labor and thrift. When capital is no longer protected as private property and is instead redefined as a communal asset, prosperity and freedom will be the greatest casualties.

Socialism always destroys wealth; it doesn't redistribute it. Unfortunately, this great truth is far from self-evident. Whether current and near retirees will stand up and fight for their retirement savings will effectively gauge the survival instinct of our country and our willingness to preserve the economic system that built it.

Notes

1. Phil Gramm and Mike Solon, "Warren's Assault on Retiree Wealth," *Wall Street Journal*, September 10, 2019, https://www.wsj.com/articles/warrens-assault-on-retiree-wealth-11568155283.

2. Pete Grieve, "Older Americans Now Own 80% of the Stock Market—Here's Why That's a Problem," Money, January 29, 2024, https://money.com/older-americans-own-most-stock-market.

3. Jesse Bricker et al., "Changes in U.S. Family Finances from 2013 to 2016: Evidence from the Survey of Consumer Finances," *Federal Reserve Bulletin* 103, no. 3 (September 2017): 13, https://www.federalreserve.gov/publications/files/scf17.pdf.

4. Employment Retirement Income Security Act of 1974, Pub. L. No. 93-406, § 404.

5. Accountable Capitalism Act, S. 3348, 115th Cong., 2nd sess., § 6 (2018).

ESG Does Neither Much Good nor Very Well

Terrence Keeley

Wall Street Journal, September 12, 2022[1]

Trillions of dollars have poured into environmental, social, and governance (ESG) funds in recent years. In 2021 alone, the figure grew $8 billion a day. Bloomberg Intelligence projects more than one-third of all globally managed assets could carry explicit ESG labels by 2025, amounting to more than $50 trillion.[2] Yet for a financial phenomenon this pervasive, there is astonishingly little evidence of its tangible benefit.

The implicit promise of ESG investing is that you can do well and do good at the same time. Investors presume they can make a market return while advancing causes such as lowering carbon emissions and addressing income inequality. But multiple studies find ESG strategies are doing little of either. Bradford Cornell of the University of California, Los Angeles, and Aswath Damodaran of New York University reviewed shareholder value created by firms with high and low ESG ratings—scores provided by professional rating agencies. Their conclusion: "Telling firms that being socially responsible will deliver higher growth, profits and value is false advertising."[3]

What Cornell and Damodaran found at the micro level is also apparent on a macro basis. Over the past five years, global ESG funds have underperformed the broader market by more than 250 basis points per year, an average 6.3 percent return compared with a 8.9 percent return.[4] This means an investor who put $10,000 into an average global ESG fund in 2017 would have about

$13,500 today, compared with the $15,250 he would have earned if he had invested in the broader market.

Did the forgone $1,750 somehow do $1,750 worth of good for mankind? Apparently not. A new report from researchers at the universities of Utah, Miami, and Hong Kong finds there is "no evidence that socially responsible investment funds improve corporate behavior."[5] But this shouldn't come as a surprise. The same outcome followed decades of investors avoiding so-called sin stocks—alcohol, tobacco, firearms, and gambling. In doing so, investors sacrificed returns while the behavior they disapproved of continued. Impact investors want their capital decisions to create outcomes that wouldn't have existed otherwise, not perpetuate the status quo.

ESG and anti-sin investing have failed for the same reason: Divestiture is an ineffective tool for generating excess returns and changing societal outcomes. It does the exact opposite of what it intends. Divestiture raises returns for the shareholders who remain invested and removes shareholders who are inclined to fight for corporate reforms. As a broad thesis, it's best to assume that products and services that can be legally and profitably delivered will be, no matter how much others disapprove of them. This includes fossil fuels. The production of goods and services declines when people stop buying them—not when others stop investing in the companies that produce them.

So what needs to change about ESG investing? To start, all ESG funds should provide impact reports with their financial returns. These reports should highlight the funds' specific "additionality," detailing the benefits it created that wouldn't have emerged otherwise. Such impact funds and reports do exist—especially in fixed income—but are a very small fraction of the overall ESG public equity market.

More fundamental makeovers are needed. Composite ESG scores—which attempt to summarize all material ESG risks into a single number or grade—convey little actionable investment information. "I have not seen circumstances where combining an analysis of E, S and G together, across a broad range of companies, . . . would facilitate meaningful investment analysis that was not significantly over-inclusive and imprecise," said former Securities and Exchange Commission (SEC) Chairman Jay Clayton during a March 2020 SEC hearing.[6] A case in point: Tesla's ESG scores by two leading rating agencies were recently below those of Pepsi.[7] Does this mean electric vehicles are worse for the planet than soft drinks or that socially concerned investors should overweight Pepsi and underweight Tesla in their portfolios?

No investment strategy, ESG or otherwise, can be any better than the data on which it is based. This is particularly true for the "S" in ESG. Social mores are constantly shifting.

Comparing credit and ESG ratings illustrates how much work lies ahead for ESG analytics. Broadly accepted financial accounting practices have enabled competing rating agents such as Fitch, S&P, and Moody's to reach similar credit evaluations 99 percent of the time. The same can't be said for their ESG counterparts, such as MSCI and Sustainalytics. In a recent paper, researchers Florian Berg, Julian Kolbel, and Roberto Rigobon found ESG scores among leading rating agencies correlated only 54 percent of the time— or barely one in two.[8] ESG ratings are all over the map because the underlying assumptions, methodologies, and data inputs vary widely among ESG rating agents.

Another area of ESG ripe for reform: disclaimers. At the end of long advertisements for popular sustainable investment funds, you'll often find something like the following: "There is no guarantee that any fund will exhibit positive or favorable sustainability characteristics." We pay more for organic food precisely because we believe it has desirable, verified characteristics. If sustainable investment funds can't be expected to exhibit favorable sustainability characteristics, they should be called something else.

ESG draws scorn from the left for being too timid and from the right for being too aggressive. The harder truth is that ESG is largely failing on its own terms. Despite tens of trillions of ESG investments, investors haven't done very well nor generated much good. ESG advocates need to do better or stop claiming they can.

Notes

1. Terrence Keeley, "ESG Does Neither Much Good nor Very Well," *Wall Street Journal*, September 12, 2022, https://www.wsj.com/articles/esg-does-neither-much-good-nor-very-well-evidence-composite-scores-impact-reports-strategy-jay-clayton-rating-agents-11663006833.

2. Bloomberg, "ESG May Surpass $41 Trillion Assets in 2022, but Not Without Challenges, Finds Bloomberg Intelligence," press release, January 24, 2022, https://www.bloomberg.com/company/press/esg-may-surpass-41-trillion-assets-in-2022-but-not-without-challenges-finds-bloomberg-intelligence.

3. Bradford Cornell and Aswath Damadoran, "Valuing ESG: Doing Good or Sounding Good?," New York University, Stern School of Business, March 20, 2020, https://papers.ssrn.com/sol3/papers.cfm?abstract_id=3557432.

4. Lauren Foster, "U.S. Sustainable Funds Underperformed in 2022. Assets Also Fell.," *Barron's*, February 22, 2023, https://www.barrons.com/articles/u-s-sustainable-funds-underpeformed-ba4aa2b8.

5. Davidson Heath et al., "Does Socially Responsible Investing Change Firm Behavior?," *Review of Finance*, European Corporate Governance Institute, and University of Miami Business School, January 18, 2023, https://papers.ssrn.com/sol3/papers.cfm?abstract_id=3837706.

6. Jay Clayton, "Remarks at Meeting of the Asset Management Advisory Committee," US Securities and Exchange Commission, May 27, 2020, https://www.sec.gov/news/public-statement/clayton-amac-opening-2020-05-27.

7. Doug Lagerstrom, "ESG | New Label, Same Problems," Private Wealth Solutions, https://www.privatewealthsolutions.com/post/esg-new-label-same-problems.

8. Florian Berg, Julian Kolbel, and Roberto Rigobon, "Aggregate Confusion: The Divergence of ESG Ratings," *Review of Finance* 26, no. 6 (November 2022): 1315–44, https://academic.oup.com/rof/article/26/6/1315/6590670.

Why ESG Funds Fail and How They Could Succeed

Terrence Keeley

Wall Street Journal, October 17, 2022[1]

Investments have consequences. Capital can be used to pursue technological breakthroughs, targeted rates of returns, or non-financial goals such as lower carbon emissions. Environmental, social, and governance (ESG) strategies have captured the imagination of many who want to do well and good—that is, generate above-market rates of return and improve social and environmental outcomes. But to date, ESG equity strategies have been broadly disappointing, underperforming common indexes while failing to generate meaningful progress against climate change. Many ESG strategies have been lose-lose.

"Temperature-aligned" funds illustrate how and why disappointment has been so common. These funds restrict investments to companies that have credibly committed to the Paris agreement goal of net-zero carbon emissions by 2050. Depending on the verification process used, 175 to 225 companies in the S&P 500 fail to meet this requirement.

In practice, this means these funds overweight sectors such as tech and finance while underweighting sectors such as oil and gas. But holding less-diversified collections of shares has neither improved risk-adjusted returns nor helped decarbonize industries. Temperature-aligned funds have financially underperformed and failed to promote a more temperature-aligned globe.

Yet there is incontestable value in having more sustainable business practices. George Serafeim of Harvard Business School estimates that sustainable companies carry a 300-basis-point equity-valuation premium over non-sustainable companies.[2] His research has two important implications. The first is that less-sustainable companies generally carry higher dividends. All else being equal, higher equity dividends will generate higher financial returns over time.

The second is that value can be created by turning "brown" companies "green." Investors who want to do well and good should target dirtier industries and companies that have the greatest transformation potential, the opposite of temperature-aligned strategies. Capital providers must invest to achieve net-zero emissions, not divest.

Lower carbon emissions aren't the only nonfinancial goals that ESG investors seek. Diversity, equity, and inclusion practices are also common, as are economic-mobility and social-justice objectives such as better primary education and health care for underserved communities.

As with climate, however, the most effective way to get corporations to improve on these objectives is through active investment and stewardship. Impact investing also differs from common ESG investing because impact investors receive transparent reports with evidence that social or environmental progress has been made. Yet less than 1 percent of all investments in equity and debt markets are explicitly made for measurable impact. This is odd because successful double-bottom-line investing isn't that hard. There are multiple investment opportunities that do well and good in a verifiable way.

Consider real assets. According to Cushman & Wakefield, mid-market offices with LEED certifications carry a 77.5 percent premium over noncertified offices.[3] Upgrading buildings from "brown" to "green" would generate significant financial value. Similarly, building renewable energy plants or government-backed low-income housing units can generate high-quality income, which would make investment portfolios more diversified and resilient. The same can be said of green, social, and sustainability-related bonds, emerging fixed-income asset classes that are growing quickly.

Venture-capital and private-equity investments dedicated to measurable impact have been shown to generate excess returns and verified social and environmental benefits, usually in terms directly linked to the United Nations Sustainable Development Goals. Bain Capital, the Sorenson Impact Foundation, TPG, Apollo Global Management, and others have been able to generate double-digit returns on mission-related investments while providing underserved populations with better housing, health care, and financial services.

Sound investment strategies consider time horizons, liquidity, risk tolerance, and impact goals. All assumed risks should be intentional, sized to desired outcomes, and thoughtfully diversified. A decision to seek verifiable impact may or may not involve explicit financial trade-offs.

If an investor wants to do well and good, ESG strategies premised on divestment are likely to disappoint. The impact-investment field has many opportunities that can generate outsized market returns and verifiable social and environmental benefits. Helping companies move from "brown" to "green" can reward your pocketbook, people, and the planet. Providing transformational housing, education, health care, digital services, and financial access to underserved communities can generate significant financial returns.

Notes

1. Terrence Keeley, "Why ESG Funds Fail, and How They Could Succeed," *Wall Street Journal*, October 17, 2022, https://www.wsj.com/articles/why-esg-funds-fail-and-how-they-could-succeed-impact-investing-financial-value-divest-dei-emissions-brown-green-11666038061.

2. George Serafeim, "Social-Impact Efforts That Create Real Value," *Harvard Business Review* (September–October 2020), https://hbr.org/2020/09/social-impact-efforts-that-create-real-value.

3. Mike Phillips, "The Facts Are In: Green Buildings Sell at Higher Values, While the Rest Decline," Bisnow, January 12, 2022, https://www.bisnow.com/london/news/sustainability/the-facts-are-in-green-buildings-sell-at-higher-values-while-the-rest-decline-111481.

The "Stakeholder Capitalism" War on the Enlightenment

Phil Gramm and Mike Solon

Wall Street Journal, May 23, 2022[1]

No one appreciated the power of capitalism more than its greatest antagonist, Karl Marx. According to Marx, capitalism, born of the Enlightenment and embodied in the Industrial Revolution, "accomplished wonders far surpassing Egyptian pyramids, Roman aqueducts, and Gothic cathedrals . . . [achieving] more massive and more colossal productive forces than have all preceding generations together" in "scarce one hundred years."[2]

Based on the erroneous notion that all value comes from labor, Marx assumed that the financier, entrepreneur, and manager were non-contributing claimants on the fruits of the worker's labor and that government could displace them and then "wither away" as growth occurred spontaneously. Most subsequent collectivists have assumed the same thing. In this utopia, workers would then receive all value created in society.

Government was never able to replicate the efficiency and innovation of private finance, entrepreneurs, and managers, and it was freedom and prosperity, not government, that always withered away. But because of the misery Marxism has imposed, the world has a living memory and therefore some natural immunity to a system in which government takes the commanding heights of the economy.

No such immunity exists to the older and therefore more dangerous socialism of the pre-Enlightenment world. In the communal world of the Dark Ages, the worker owed fealty to crown, church, guild, and village. Those "stakeholders" extracted a share of the product of the sweat of the worker's brow and the fruits of his thrift. Growth stagnated as the rewards for effort and thrift were leached away.

The 18th-century Enlightenment liberated mind, soul, and property, empowering people to think their own thoughts and ultimately have a voice in their government, worship as they chose, and own the fruits of their own labor and thrift. As Enlightenment economist Adam Smith put it, "The property which every man has in his own labour, as it is the original foundation of all property, so it is the most sacred and inviolable."[3]

The British Parliament repealed royal charters, permitted businesses to incorporate simply by meeting preset capital requirements, and established the rules of law governing private competition. Most important, laws were made through a process of open deliberation with public votes. This democratic process replaced the intimidation of medieval stakeholders, who under the communal concept of labor and capital took a share of what others produced.

These Enlightenment ideas spawned the Industrial Revolution and gave birth to the modern world, as described by Marx. As people sought their own advancement under a system of private property and the rule of law, as if guided by Smith's "invisible hand," they promoted the public interest without intention or knowledge of doing so. Freedom and self-interest unleashed the world's greatest productive effort and continue to drive progress to this day.

The pre-Enlightenment world was dominated by the powerful, who defined the public interest to benefit themselves and imposed their will on productive members of society. When labor and capital are forced to share what they produce with stakeholders, the reward for working and saving is plundered.

In the post-Enlightenment world, people were empowered to pursue their own private interests. Private interests and free markets accomplished what no benevolent king's redistribution, no loving bishop's charity, no mercantilistic protectionism, and no powerful guild ever did—broad, unending prosperity.

Remarkably, amid the recorded successes of capitalism and failures of socialism rooted in Marxism, pre-Enlightenment socialism is reemerging in the name of stakeholder capitalism. These stakeholders claim that "you did not build your business" and that your labor and thrift should serve their definition of the public interest.

The initial target of this extortion is corporate America. Stakeholders argue that rich capitalists who own big businesses already get more than they deserve. But since roughly 70 percent of corporate revenues go to labor,[4] the biggest losers in stakeholder capitalism are workers, whose wages will be cannibalized.

And of course, the idea that rich capitalists own corporate America is largely a progressive myth. Some 72 percent of the value of publicly traded companies in America is owned by pensions, 401(k)s, individual retirement accounts, charitable organizations, and insurance companies funding life insurance policies and annuities.[5] The overwhelming majority of involuntary sharers in stakeholder capitalism will be workers and retirees.

The mantra that private wealth must serve the public interest has been boosted by one of capitalism's great innovations, the index fund. What investors gained in the efficiency of the index fund's low fees, they are now losing as index funds use the extraordinary voting power they possess in voting other people's shares. Whether their motives are promoting the marketing of their index funds, doing "good" with other people's money, or, as Warren Buffett's longtime partner Charlie Munger claimed, playing "emperor,"[6] they have empowered the environmental, social, and governance (ESG) agenda. Other stakeholders are sure to pile on, as evidenced by Sens. Bernie Sanders (I-VT) and Elizabeth

Warren's (D-MA) effort to get BlackRock to use its share-voting power to pressure a private company to yield to union demands.[7] Stakeholder capitalism imperils more than prosperity; it imperils democracy itself. Self-proclaimed stakeholders demand that workers and investors serve their interests even though no law has been enacted imposing the ESG agenda.

Fiduciary laws require those entrusted with investors' money to use it "solely in the interest of . . . [and] for the exclusive purpose of providing benefits" to the investor.[8] The index funds that enable stakeholders to intimidate public boards are violating federal fiduciary requirements, and those government agencies that enforce stakeholder capitalism are engaged in an unconstitutional takings under the Fifth Amendment of the Constitution.

In our post-Enlightenment world, public interests beyond the confluence of private interests are defined by the public actions of a constitutionally constrained government. By overturning the Enlightenment, stakeholder capitalism endangers not only capitalism and prosperity but democracy and freedom as well.

Notes

1. Phil Gramm and Mike Solon, "The 'Stakeholder Capitalism' War on the Enlightenment," *Wall Street Journal*, May 23, 2022, https://www.wsj.com/articles/stakeholder-capitalism-enlightenment-blackrock-esg-index-fund-passive-invest-elizabeth-warren-bernie-sanders-retirement-11653313715.

2. Karl Marx, "Manifesto of the Communist Party," in *Great Books of the Western World*, ed. Robert Maynard Hutchins (Encyclopedia Britannica, 1952), 50:421.

3. Adam Smith, "Chapter X: On Wages and Profit in the Different Employments of Labour and Stock," Marxists Internet Archive, https://www.marxists.org/reference/archive/smith-adam/works/wealth-of-nations/book01/ch10b.htm.

4. Paycor, "The Biggest Cost of Doing Business: A Closer Look at Labor Costs," December 8, 2022, https://www.paycor.com/resource-center/articles/closer-look-at-labor-costs; and HCMI, "TCOW—Total Cost of Workforce," https://www.hcmi.co/tcow-total-cost-of-workforce.

5. Steven M. Rosenthal and Lydia S. Austin, "The Dwindling Taxable Share of U.S. Corporate Stock," *Tax Notes*, May 16, 2016, https://www.urban.org/sites/default/files/publication/80621/2000790-The-Dwindling-Taxable-Share-of-U.S.-Corporate-Stock.pdf.

6. Editorial Board, "Calling Out 'Emperor' Larry Fink," *Wall Street Journal*, February 17, 2022, https://www.wsj.com/articles/calling-out-emperor-larry-fink-charlie-munger-financial-markets-berkshire-hathaway-11645136040.

7. Thomas Franck and Ylan Mui, "Sanders, Warren and Baldwin Urge Larry Fink to Intervene in Strike at Coal Company Partially Owned by BlackRock," CNBC, January 14, 2022, https://www.cnbc.com/2022/01/14/bernie-sanders-elizabeth-warren-urge-blackrock-ceo-larry-fink-to-intervene-in-coal-strike.html.

8. US Department of Labor, "Fiduciary Responsibilities," https://www.dol.gov/general/topic/retirement/fiduciaryresp.

The Securities and Exchange Commission Seeks to Supplant the Market

Phil Gramm and Hester Peirce

Wall Street Journal, January 19, 2023[1]

When the financial crisis ended in the summer of 2009, economic prognosticators were virtually unanimous in predicting a strong, sustained recovery. But Obama-era regulatory policy smothered that recovery and made it the weakest since the Great Depression.

Now, with the economy expected to slip into recession, the coming regulatory tsunami far exceeds the excesses of the post-financial-crisis period. Nowhere are the current regulatory excesses more evident than at the Securities and Exchange Commission (SEC).

The SEC's mandate is vital but limited. Securities laws empower the commission to combat market abuses and fraud and to ensure that investors have material information to make their own investment judgments. As President Franklin D. Roosevelt explained when signing the Securities Act of 1933:

> It is, of course, no insurance against errors of judgment. That is the function of no Government. It does give assurance, however, that, within the limit of its powers, the Federal Government will insist upon knowledge of the facts on which alone judgment can be based.[2]

But the SEC now proposes to substitute its own judgment for that of investors, corporate directors, and managers. Its recent set of proposed rules, many of which go beyond any statutory remit, have little to do with preventing abuse or fostering transparency. The SEC has taken on the role of telling companies how to run themselves and investors how to invest. In the process, the SEC is eviscerating the vital barrier in our market-driven economy between the limited and legally constrained responsibilities of the public sector and the primacy of the private sector as the driver of American prosperity.

Consider the commission's climate-change proposal,[3] which seeks to force climate risk to the center of every public company's boardroom and management discussion. It would push companies to populate their boards and management ranks with climate experts and focus their strategic business and financial plans away from increasing market share and profitability to plans to transition to a lower-carbon economy.

Although technically applicable only to public companies, the proposal would reach every customer and supplier in a public company's "value chain." Large public companies would have to collect and report their suppliers' and customers' greenhouse-gas emissions, forcing countless small businesses and farmers to undertake expensive guessing exercises about how much of seven different gases they might be emitting.

The SEC, in a tacit acknowledgment of the proposed rule's compliance burdens, moonlights in the proposal as a management consultant. It suggests that one way to reduce the data-collection burden is to work with "suppliers and downstream distributors to take steps to reduce those entities' . . . emissions."[4] The SEC also suggests that public companies make "products that are more energy efficient or involve less emissions when consumers use them," choose "distributors that use shorter transportation routes," or "purchase from more [greenhouse gas] efficient suppliers."[5]

The SEC proposes to turn a disclosure rule into a how-to guide for companies seeking to reduce their carbon footprints. Inducing private companies to take specific steps to meet unlegislated social goals has nothing to do with achieving the SEC's mission of combating fraud, increasing transparency, and fostering market integrity. It would undermine the market efficiency that the SEC's rules are supposed to support.

The commission also proposes to disrupt the mutual-funds market. Long a staple of retail investors' portfolios, mutual funds are a cheap and effective way to gain diversified, liquid exposure to the markets. A recent SEC proposal would fundamentally change mutual funds.

The market already offers exchange-traded funds for investors who are concerned that their funds will be diluted when other shareholders sell, but the SEC insists that mutual funds be redesigned to address this concern. Although presented as an investor-protection measure, the proposal could harm retail investors. Funds would be forced to use a complicated pricing formula and impose a surcharge on investors trying to buy and sell fund shares, which would require a costly redesign of the entire mutual-fund distribution system. The SEC itself acknowledges the proposal would increase mutual-fund investors' costs, decrease their convenience, and even drive investors out of mutual funds altogether. The commission seems willing to jeopardize one of our most successful investment products based solely on the premise that it understands markets better than market participants do.

A well-functioning equity market is fundamental to a healthy economy. Here, too, the SEC proposes to fix what appears not to be broken. Retail investors can buy and sell stocks more easily than ever before, at competitive prices, often without paying a commission. Rather than simply work to enhance existing disclosures, the SEC has decided to remake the markets by forcing retail orders into auctions of its own design. Allowing the market to experiment with auctions would be fine, but the SEC wants to force all retail investors into those auctions. In so doing, the SEC proposes to replace the judgment of retail brokers about how to best serve their customers with its own one-size-fits-all model for executing stock trades.

The SEC not only has expanded its regulatory reach far beyond its legal authority; it has morphed from an umpire objectively enforcing the rule of law to an economic policymaker dictating how the economy will operate. The SEC's rule proposals would change the way companies are managed and the way investors invest. Government prescriptions, not private preferences, would decide how Americans' hard-earned money is put to work. Reflecting a conceit that its judgment is superior to the collective wisdom of the market, the SEC proposes to expand the role of government and reduce the economic freedom that has been the source of American economic exceptionalism.

Notes

1. Phil Gramm and Hester Peirce, "The SEC Seeks to Supplant the Market," *Wall Street Journal*, January 19, 2023, https://www.wsj.com/articles/the-sec-seeks-to-supplant-the-market-11674159388.

2. Franklin D. Roosevelt, "Statement on Signing the Securities Bill," American Presidency Project, May 27, 1933, https://www.presidency.ucsb.edu/documents/statement-signing-the-securities-bill.

3. US Securities and Exchange Commission, "SEC Proposes Rules to Enhance and Standardize Climate-Related Disclosures for Investors," press release, March 21, 2022, https://www.sec.gov/news/press-release/2022-46.

4. US Securities and Exchange Commission, "The Enhancement and Standardization of Climate-Related Disclosures for Investors," *Federal Register* 87, no. 69 (April 11, 2022): 21377, https://www.govinfo.gov/content/pkg/FR-2022-04-11/pdf/2022-06342.pdf.

5. Hester Peirce, "We Are Not the Securities and Environment Commission—at Least Not Yet," US Securities and Exchange Commission, March 21, 2022, https://www.sec.gov/news/statement/peirce-climate-disclosure-20220321.

How Conservatives Can Get ESG Right

Terrence Keeley

National Review, January 25, 2023[1]

The senior editor of *American Affairs*, Julius Krein, was unsparing in his criticism of conservatives in his recent article "Why the Right Can't Beat ESG." "Conservatives' purely negative approach to ESG, coupled with a naïve desire to return to older forms of shareholder primacy, will prove counterproductive," he concludes, bemoaning "the absence of any substantive alternative agenda."[2]

Krein does a good job highlighting how and why persistent Republican potshots against ESG have failed to rein in a beast that has done more harm than good. ESG has become a religion for many. That it has morphed into a hotbed of political controversy rather than a constructive conversation about the pros and cons of sustainable investment says more about our tribal psychology than it does about ESG. Jonathan Haidt can explain the broader phenomenon behind this if you're interested.[3]

But conservatives mustn't give up the fight. ESG remains a fatally flawed investment paradigm. It is premised on unreliable data and the dangerous, highly misleading idea that tilting away from certain shares or bonds will fundamentally alter corporate behavior, improve risk-adjusted returns, and result in better social and environmental outcomes. None of these claims is true. Getting ESG right requires identifying how and where mindful corporate practice and investment generate true, double bottom lines. All the rest is hokum. Discernment like this transcends politics, however. ESG's strengths and weaknesses don't change if your state is red, blue, or purple. Politicians of all colors should unite in deriding investment strategies that don't help asset owners achieve their intended goals. But conservatives mustn't overreach either. In a country where "best interest" regulation is the law of the land, investors are empowered to make their own investment decisions, however flimsy those decisions may be. Regulators should intervene if there is insufficient market competition or faulty disclosures. Beyond that, it's caveat emptor. There is no law against foolish capital allocation, even though dumb financial decisions are common when politics are prioritized over value creation and risk mitigation.

Consider Democrat Brad Lander, New York City's comptroller. He recently lambasted BlackRock for not forcing its clients to buy more of the ineffectual products he endorses, so-called temperature-aligned funds.[4] Temperature-aligned funds exclude all firms that are not compliant with the Paris agreement. They neither affect the globe's temperature nor generate better risk-adjusted investment outcomes. Lander should know the earth would still be on course for a temperature increase well beyond the 2050 net-zero goal of the Paris accord even if every portfolio on the planet were temperature-aligned. To decarbonize industry, transportation, housing, agriculture, and the grid, we must invest in dirty industries, not divest. Lander has flipped the sustainable-investment challenge on its head.

But Democrats are not alone in being led astray by ESG. Texas Comptroller Glenn Hegar, a Republican, has also blundered. In defense of the Lone Star State's economy, Hegar pledged to boycott financial firms that boycott energy but then did the exact opposite.[5] He blacklisted some of the most important investors in energy in Texas, increasing borrowing costs for Texan oil corporations and taxpayers in the process. Hegar and Lander don't share political ideologies, but they have something else in common: Both let their political beliefs impede sound financial judgment. Politics and markets should be like church and state: as separate as possible.

Krein is not just calling for a conservative reckoning on ESG, though. He yearns for something broader, more comprehensive. Addressing ESG's flaws "will require abandoning the silly pretense that 'the market' is a magical, perfect, self-regulating machine of 18th-century deism, operating independently of politics and society," he insists. "It will require the intellectual awareness and discipline to pragmatically incorporate these goals into constructive policy and corporate governance frameworks."[6]

As a conservative, I must note Krein is already on heretical ground with his criticisms. Conservatives don't defend markets because they are perfect: We do so because they are better at allocating capital and identifying growth opportunities than government agents who claim to know better. What Krein should have said is that conservatives recognize markets are essential, but they too often ignore their negative externalities. Conservatives must combine their valid defense of free markets with pragmatic, effective plans to countervail their failures. Today, those failures include environmental degradation and social contracts increasingly strained by widening wealth gaps. These are, after all, primarily what the "E" (environmental) and "S" (social) in ESG are all about.

Krein would be right to highlight market failures and the absence of comprehensive Republican plans to deal with them. Conservatives should respond thoughtfully to all valid environmental and social concerns. Modern capitalism taxes our air, water, and land in detrimental ways. Overwhelming evidence suggests current consumption and production patterns are contributing to the extinction of many insects and animals, while potentially rendering unlivable certain densely inhabited environs, including whole cities and several island nation-states. None of this is political; the evidence is there for all to see.

On the other hand, anyone who claims to know what the temperature of the earth will be in 50–100 years and why we must spend $100 trillion to change it is deceiving himself. The same holds true for sea levels. Global temperatures could be higher or lower. Nonhuman influences caused the earth's last mass-extinction event by making it much colder. Seas aren't rising very fast and may not do so anytime soon. The future timing of non-anthropogenic events remains unknown and unknowable.

But the temperature of the earth and sea levels decades from now are not our political problems at hand—or, at least, they shouldn't be. As the global population will soon top out around 10 billion, left and right alike must think long and hard about how every human soul will be able to live sustainably and in a manner consistent with the inherent dignities bestowed by their divine maker. We must also ask why growing numbers of highly capable people are not reaching their full potential. In so doing, we must remain crystal clear about the precise roles individuals, civil society, policymakers, business, finance, regulators, and public policy can and cannot play in optimizing outcomes.

Individual behaviors are key. Business and finance have no special powers to turn the carbon clock backward or reverse decades of racial and gender discrimination; consumer choices and public policies drive outcomes far more determinately. Financiers and corporate CEOs are not, nor should they ever be, social- or environmental-justice warriors, forever prioritizing stakeholders at the long-run expense of their shareholders. This is not their job, legally or ethically.

If every corporate enterprise substituted a range of E and S goals for their growth opportunities, the global economy would experience a catastrophic growth shock, far worse than the COVID-19 shutdown. When per capita growth falters, human misery quickly mounts, especially for the poor. Lawlessness, mass migration, and unconstrained environmental desecration invariably multiply when economies fail. Calls for renewed economic growth would soon rise in a cacophonic frenzy. If we want to make the world more environmentally sustainable and socially inclusive, we will need to spend more money—perhaps as much as $275 trillion over the next 40 years by some estimates.[7] Exactly where would these funds come from in a global economy experiencing free fall?

None of this means business and finance should remain oblivious to the changing priorities of our times—but neither can they do so and thrive. This may be what Krein meant when he wrote, "The business of business is never just business."[8] Business and finance exist in their primary incarnation to serve the broad interests of society. Their sine qua non is to generate economic growth. If business and finance do not generate economic growth, nothing else will.

As it so happens, good business practice and many ESG priorities are increasingly, though not perfectly, aligning. Companies today fail their shareowners if they ignore the interests of their employees, their suppliers, their community, and the environment. This is not stakeholder capitalism, though; it's just capitalism. Conservatives not only celebrate market-driven innovations that result in material, social, environmental, and spiritual progress; because we understand markets, we expect them.

Krein also deserves credit for highlighting the need for a comprehensive, conservative road map that could credibly solve the real problems of our day. Republicans need a road map that would enable society to get all the good out of ESG without the bad—and much else besides.

But progressives need a workable ESG road map, too. Blind acceptance of ESG precepts has resulted in trillions of dollars of misallocated capital and zero progress toward its principal target, climate change. Doubling down on failing ESG methods is nuts. Its merits and risks aren't red, blue, or purple; they are black and white. When it comes to optimizing commercial and financial outcomes, color-tinted lenses impede clear thinking. If we prioritize principles over politics, all our road maps will align.

Promoting the broadest levels of human flourishing ethically, effectively, and for as long as humanly possible requires these five core tenets to serve as our pillars.

1. Let Markets Work

Years of naming and shaming public oil and gas companies while billions of consumers continued to rely on their products ended predictably: massive energy shortages and dangerous dependence on Vladimir Putin, who promptly pounced on Ukraine. Ignoring the laws of supply and demand encourages such tragedies. After natural gas prices in Europe jumped tenfold versus 2018, clean-energy investments topped $1.4 trillion in 2022, a record.[9] No surprise here either. Wind, solar, geothermal, and nuclear energy are now cheaper than fossil fuels, in Europe at least. As the need for more domestically sourced energy has simultaneously jumped, all energy sources are finally receiving the investments they need. Putin's horrific crime accomplished precisely what the *gilets jaunes* in France democratically precluded: an effective carbon tax.

Similarly, if Citigroup CEO Jane Fraser has found that flexible work hours and locations provide her with a more committed workforce, while David Solomon at Goldman Sachs has found the exact opposite, both can be right. Price and non-price incentives are essential to sound decision-making and free-market solutions. Abandoning market discipline delays, and ultimately compounds, human woes. Disallowing free-market competition stifles creativity, innovation, and entrepreneurship, each of which are essential for enduring prosperity.

Friedrich Hayek said it best: "I regard the preservation of what is known as the capitalist system, of the system of free markets and the private ownership of the means of production, as an essential condition of the very survival of mankind."[10] We must allow markets to be free to survive.

2. Recognize That Consumer, Worker, and Societal Attitudes Change

Occidental Petroleum's visionary CEO Vicki Hollub has discovered a growth market: carbon-neutral oil. Once the world's largest carbon-capture facility is complete, Oxy Low Carbon Ventures will have virtually unlimited demand for its cleanest fossil fuel. Carbon-neutral oil can power private planes, generate electricity while wind and sun are missing, and enable companies that have committed to net-zero emissions to achieve their goals efficiently. But none of this is "woke." It's simply capitalism.

Similarly, high-quality synthetic leather will be a $65 billion market by 2030, up more than 1,000 percent from 2022.[11] High-end, faux-leather goods made from mycelium—a natural product derived from mushroom roots—verifiably claim to be carbon negative, the opposite of methane-rich, bovine-derived traditional leather products. Gen Z shoppers are leading the way in increased spending on these types of "sustainable" products. On balance, their wallets are driving up demand while the consumption of traditional apparel, footwear, and accessories has fallen 20 percent since 2019.[12]

Of course, many boomers, Gen Xers, and millennials are conditioned toward less mindful consumption patterns, and their demands must be met too. Younger consumers and workers coupled with a growing number of well-heeled older folk have evolving expectations, hopes, and dreams. A growing number realize the earth has never had to support 8–10 billion human inhabitants before. Before too long, everyone will. Emerging preferences for circular production and sustainable products are natural, market-driven phenomena. They will intensify over time.

3. Double Down on Shareowner Primacy

"In a free-enterprise, private-property system, a corporate executive is an employee of the owners of the business."[13] So wrote Nobel laureate Milton Friedman in his sensational 1970 essay "The Social Responsibility of Business Is to Increase Its Profits." I know very few conservatives who would debate Friedman on this—and none who should. Anyone who believes a business should be run for the benefit of someone other than its owners must read the 1919 Michigan Supreme Court opinion by Russell Ostrander, *Dodge v. Ford Motor Company.* There, he or she will learn shareowner primacy isn't just sound practice: It's also the law of the land.

Protesters campaigning outside corporate offices should be respectfully told that their concerns are laudable but their energies would be better spent buying shares and waging proxy fights. Those same protesters should be graciously asked how they'd feel if some stranger came into their home and told them to change their appliances, drapes, and furniture. After all, that is effectively what they are demanding of the corporations they are protesting.

Businesses are run by and for the benefit of their owners, subject to local and international law. Those owners also bear risks and responsibilities, neither of which are negligible. There are ways to change corporate behaviors legally and responsibly. There is just no way to reassign those controls to some newly empowered, nondemocratic agent and still be a conservative.

4. Recognize Shareowners' Priorities Are Changing Too

Friedman never claimed that corporations should merely prioritize short-term profitability. In the same 1970 article, he wrote that companies should "make as much money as possible while conforming to the basic rules of the society, both those embodied in law and those embodied in ethical custom."[14] Over the past half century, shareowners have repeatedly rejected the short-term preferences of management when their long-term welfare has been imperiled. Increasingly, long-term shareholder welfare is becoming embodied in our laws and ethical customs.

In the 1980s, shareowners instituted executive-pay guidelines and poison-pill-takeover protections. In the early 1990s, they voted to remove the CEOs at Westinghouse, American Express, IBM, Kodak, and General Motors. More recently, shareowners forced Wendy's to join the fair-food program and DuPont to account for the long-term disposal of the 10 trillion plastic pellets they manufacture annually. All these measures have the same cause and effect: Shareowners are instructing managers of the companies they own to incur short-term costs in exchange for what they believe will lead to long-term gains.

This trend now appears to be accelerating, with more environmental and social concerns rising. Why? Because the demographics of shareowners are shifting to pensioners who want the value of their investments to be maximized over 25–30 years, not 25–30 days. Growing numbers of shareowner resolutions seeking lower carbon emissions or increased workforce diversity make sense in this context. What retiree wants to live in a world with unbreathable air, undrinkable water, and whole segments of society underemployed? If most shareowners say they want every employee of Walmart to have access to GED certification, free college tuition, and books—which they now do—what non-shareowner has the right to stop them?

Krein says, "Conservatives should develop their own investment frameworks."[15] Conservatives already have an investment framework: whatever a majority of shareowners of a specific company decides. Study the history of corporate governance closely. You'll see shareowners have repeatedly asserted their rights in important, evolving ways. There is no practical alternative to shareowner primacy. Neither progressives nor conservatives have the right to cry foul when they feel that primacy is abused. Today, virtually anyone can buy a few shares of a company and fight openly for more sensible strategies. Competition in corporate governance is partly what led Vivek Ramaswamy to start Strive Asset Management. In time, this debate will sort itself out. Nothing would be more un-conservative than claiming there should be one, new, transfixed investment framework. There should be multiple competing ones, so asset owners can exercise informed choice.

5. Prioritize Efficient Remediation Policies That Work

And now we come to the "remediate negative externalities" part, the part where conservatives have been weakest. Fortunately, our tools and opportunities here are multitudinous.

Consider the Lab for Economic Opportunities (LEO) at the University of Notre Dame.[16] This group of nonpartisan academics is on a mission: to outsmart poverty. Rigorous data analysis has led them to many counterintuitive conclusions. To lower adolescent-recidivism rates, teach Aristotelian ethics to high school dropouts. To multiply accreditation rates in community colleges, provide enrolled, unwed mothers free caseworker counseling. And to match education with employment opportunities more optimally, stop telling everyone to go to college. There are tens of thousands of reliable career pathways in the information-technology industry. Most can be accessed through tuition-free certification programs.

Similarly, the Environmental Defense Fund (EDF) has helped dozens of US corporations save more than $1.6 billion in energy costs while boosting their operational efficiency.[17] For example, EDF showed McDonald's how to reduce its packaging and waste by 30 percent while saving millions of dollars annually. EDF is changing industrial-scale farming and fishing in ways that will enable growing populations to feed themselves forever, even as climate changes.

What do these two powerful, remediating organizations illustrate—the first social, the second environmental? First, that sensible solutions are neither red nor blue: They are simply sensible. Second, that many of our best policy solutions have not been discovered or mandated by Krein's new government. Rather, they have come out of private industry and America's vibrant, globe-leading nongovernmental organization ecosystem.

LEO and EDF are what I call "Exemplars of Hope."[18] Exemplars of Hope are nongovernmental organizations or other civic service organizations that have scalable programs and methodologies that verifiably promote more inclusive, sustainable economic growth. The world we all hope to inhabit would be advanced by their successful propagation. Evidence-based programs that promote more inclusive, more sustainable economic growth are highly effective ways of countervailing two of the most pernicious negative externalities of modern capitalism: environmental degradation and strained social contracts. They can and should be complemented with a broad expansion of public-private partnerships and private impact investments—that is, capital commitments that generate superior returns and verifiable social and environmental advances. My research shows the "do well–do good" private investment market may be as large as $6 trillion per year.[19] Private impact investments on this scale would be more than enough to achieve all the United Nations Sustainable Development Goals by 2035, should that be the direction voters insist we go.

Conclusion

Of course, none of the five principles above are meant to preclude thorough debates about broader public policy changes. Adherence to these five principles would forge more optimal economic, environmental, and societal outcomes. This said, more work is needed to discern optimal corporate-tax rates, sensible worker-apprenticeship programs, and the lasting benefits of charter-school choice, among other policies. Krein's challenge was specific to ESG, however. He said the right can't "beat" ESG. If you've gotten this far, you probably believe ESG is a thing worth beating, or at least dealing with sternly. I do as well. ESG has done more harm than good. It has misled millions of investors into thinking that the way to transform our industries, live more sustainably, and still enjoy abundance is to tilt and time public equity weightings in a portfolio relative to standard indexes like the S&P 500. They are wrong. The world would be far better without these misconceptions. In the interests of ESG's speedy demise and my conservative beliefs, however, allow me to suggest another course of action.

Remember the BRIC phenomenon that began in 2001? We were all repeatedly told to prioritize Brazil, Russia, India, and China in our portfolios. By the time the global financial crisis rolled around a few years later, these four countries had become irreconcilable bedfellows. Who wants to invest in Russia now? Similarly, FANG became FAANG before markets broke up the band. Today, no one believes Facebook (Meta), Apple, Amazon, Netflix, and Google are essential building blocks of a sound portfolio.

Acronym-based investment fads invariably burn themselves out. The same is already happening with ESG. Its persistent underperformance and fading credibility as an investment paradigm have shown all who can see that ESG is failing on its own terms.[20] Professional calls for ESG advocates to produce more compelling evidence about the longer-run resilience of their products have gone unanswered for a reason: There is no such evidence.[21]

At a minimum, ESG as an investment paradigm needs a divorce. E, S, and G became conjoined because the original United Nations Principles for Responsible Investment proposed that they should. No rigorous analysis was ever conducted about their combined salience. The case for their immediate disaggregation is irrefutable.

I believe ESG will soon go the same way as BRIC and FAANG. We are witnessing an investment fad in terminal decline.

But what's the real lesson in this, most especially for conservatives? It's not just that all acronym-based investment strategies are specious. Rather, it's that sticking to our principles over the long run works. It also lets a lot of Sturm und Drang simply blow over. Conservatives and progressives should both point out ESG's inconsistencies and failures, but neither should be goaded into more time-consuming fights, especially when our energies are so badly needed elsewhere.

Which brings me to the far more important topic of energy reliability and independence. Instead of debating whether ESG was good yesterday, today, or tomorrow, can we please finish building critical oil and gas pipelines in California and West Virginia so that their residents get the power they need to thrive? The private capital is ready: As you'd expect, they are only waiting for government permits.

And remember, solving real human problems efficiently is what true conservatism is all about.

Notes

1. Terrence Keeley, "How Conservatives Can Get ESG Right," *National Review*, January 25, 2023, https://www.nationalreview.com/2023/01/how-conservatives-can-get-esg-right.

2. Julius Krein, "Why the Right Can't Beat ESG," Compact, January 3, 2023, https://www.compactmag.com/article/why-the-right-can-t-beat-esg.

3. Jonathan Haidt, *The Righteous Mind: Why Good People Are Divided by Politics and Religion* (New York: Pantheon Books, 2012).

4. Brad Lander, letter to Laurence D. Fink, September 21, 2022, https://comptroller.nyc.gov/wp-content/uploads/2022/09/Letter-to-BlackRock-CEO-Larry-Fink.pdf.

5. Texas Comptroller of Public Accounts, "Texas Comptroller Glenn Hegar Announces List of Financial Companies That Boycott Energy Companies," press release, August 24, 2022, https://comptroller.texas.gov/about/media-center/news/20220824-texas-comptroller-glenn-hegar-announces-list-of-financial-companies-that-boycott-energy-companies-1661267815099.

6. Krein, "Why the Right Can't Beat ESG."

7. McKinsey Global Institute, *The Net-Zero Transition: What It Would Cost, What It Could Bring*, January 2022, https://www.mckinsey.com/capabilities/sustainability/our-insights/the-net-zero-transition-what-it-would-cost-what-it-could-bring.

8. Krein, "Why the Right Can't Beat ESG."

9. Nathaniel Bullard, "Clean Energy Sets $1.1 Trillion Record That's Bound to Be Broken," Bloomberg, January 26, 2023, https://www.bloomberg.com/news/articles/2023-01-26/clean-energy-fossil-fuel-investment-tied-for-first-time-in-2022.

10. Larry Kudlow, "Hayek on Capitalism," *National Review*, April 23, 2007, https://www.nationalreview.com/kudlows-money-politics/hayek-capitalism-larry-kudlow.

11. Grand View Research, *Synthetic Leather Market Size: Market Analysis 2018–2030*, 2023, https://www.grandviewresearch.com/industry-analysis/synthetic-leather-market.

12. Daphne Howland, "Consumers Are Hitting the Brakes on Apparel Purchases: UBS," Retail Dive, December 21, 2022, https://www.retaildive.com/news/consumers-spend-less-apparel-store-closures/639258.

13. Milton Friedman, "The Social Responsibility of Business Is to Increase Its Profits," *New York Times*, September 13, 1970, https://www.nytimes.com/1970/09/13/archives/a-friedman-doctrine-the-social-responsibility-of-business-is-to.html.

14. Friedman, "The Social Responsibility of Business Is to Increase Its Profits."

15. Krein, "Why the Right Can't Beat ESG."

16. University of Notre Dame, Wilson Sheehan Lab for Economic Opportunities, website, https://leo.nd.edu.

17. Environmental Defense Fund, "Our Work: Delivering Bold Climate Change Solutions," https://www.edf.org/our-work.

18. 1PointSix, website, https://www.1pointsix.com.

19. Terrence Keeley, *Sustainable: Moving Beyond ESG to Impact Investing* (New York: Columbia University Press, 2022), chaps. 16 and 17.

20. Terrence Keeley, "ESG Does Neither Much Good nor Very Well," *Wall Street Journal*, September 12, 2022, https://www.wsj.com/articles/esg-does-neither-much-good-nor-very-well-evidence-composite-scores-impact-reports-strategy-jay-clayton-rating-agents-11663006833.

21. Terrence Keeley, "ESG Is Unsustainable," Ignites, November 28, 2022, https://www.ignites.com/c/3836154/496694.

ESG Must Evolve into Something Less Politically Explosive Than ESG

Terrence Keeley

RealClearMarkets, June 7, 2023[1]

Can something be both vital *and* flawed?

This was the fundamental question of the public debate I had last week with Professor Witold Henisz, the vice dean of the Wharton School of the University of Pennsylvania. We were invited by *The Economist* to battle Oxford-style over the following motion: "This House believes ESG is vital and a necessity in the battle against climate change." The debate, energetically moderated by Vijay Vaitheeswaran, *The Economist*'s global energy and climate innovation editor, was billed as one of the highlights of the magazine's Third Annual Sustainability Week.[2] Dean Henisz argued in favor of the motion. I argued against.

In the end, we found profound areas of both agreement and disagreement. The day before, in another panel, Dean Henisz said, "We have a long way to go before ESG products are fit for purpose." I latched on to his damning critique, telling the audience that Henisz could not have it both ways: That is, he cannot claim ESG is both vital and unfit. He shrewdly returned the tactic, quoting excerpts from several of my recent podcasts and new book *Sustainable: Moving Beyond ESG to Impact Investing.* "We should all want the ethos of ESG to reign," I have written.[3]

So, which is it? And most importantly, how do we salvage the good of ESG while ridding ourselves of its defects?

Nothing less than a radically honest approach will work. This means first accepting that the ESG movement has valid precepts. Business and finance have crucial roles to play in fashioning optimal environmental, economic, and social outcomes. Current consumption and industrial production patterns are despoiling our air, land, and water in visibly detrimental, perhaps even cataclysmic, ways. Moreover, years of rapid economic growth have widened wealth gaps and severely strained social contracts. Correcting these negative effects requires urgent action from all pillars of society—not only individuals, regulators, and civic organizations but also corporations and investors.

We must also remember how ESG was born. ESG investing grew out of the United Nations' Principles for Responsible Investment.[4] A group of global financial experts assembled by former UN Secretary-General Kofi Annan studied how investors could be more mindful about addressing the unique challenges and opportunities of the 21st century and simultaneously more supportive of the UN's Sustainable Development Goals (SDGs).[5] In 2004, these experts concluded rightly that all investors should systematically incorporate ESG material-risk considerations into their decision-making.

From these two prompts, multiple initiatives have taken root. Like medieval alchemists, who believed that gold could somehow be derived from base metals, many well-intended financial alchemists like MSCI, Sustainalytics, Morningstar, and Bloomberg have endeavored to prove there is some predictive and prescriptive capacity in these three variables, E, S, and G. Collectively, they have spent millions of hours and dollars to prove that their unique, analytic ESG processes and investment products could outperform the broader market and promote the UN SDGs.

But here's yet another hard truth: All these efforts have failed. As my research and that of many others has exhaustively shown,[6] ESG investment products are not generating consistent financial performance. Neither are they producing much good—almost none that would not have taken place if ESG had never been born, that is.[7]

And this is where the debate gets most interesting. Is ESG failing to perform as hoped because we aren't trying hard enough, haven't spent enough time, or haven't conducted the right tests—or is something more vexing at work? Dean Henisz thinks the former. I believe it's the latter.

Note, however, what's not at issue. Neither of us believe that the broad claims of the UN's Principles for Responsible Investment are wrong. Governance, environmental, and social factors present material risks. This claim is often made most demonstrably by activists who shout, "Climate risk is investment risk!" Yes, it is. But is climate risk, along with other S and G risks, fundamentally *mispriced*? If so, over what time frame? Moreover, won't other factors continue to affect asset prices at the same time? What about a corporation's capacity to innovate and transform? Don't corporate culture, management quality, and financial efficacy also matter? And mightn't these factors frequently overwhelm ESG considerations?

And while we're at it, how about other unknowable things, like Vladimir Putin's war in Ukraine, stubborn human dependence on coal and other fossil fuels, a US debt-ceiling crisis, and China's potential invasion of Taiwan? There is simply no way that all these factors are less important than environmental and social risks.

Unemotional reflections like these make the obvious more evident. There's nothing special about E, S, or G that axiomatically elevates them in asset-price determination. This is why Vanguard CEO Tim Buckley recently said that ESG investing provides no advantage over broad index investing.[8] It is also why Professor Alex Edmans of the London Business School has called for the end of ESG. "ESG doesn't need a specialized term," Professor Edmans writes. "It's no better or worse than other intangible assets that drive long-term value and create positive externalities for wider society."[9]

Value-producing strategies "can deliver financial returns and societal impacts," Dean Henisz wrote after our debate.[10] I agree. "ESG integration still offers tremendous potential to investors."[11] Indeed, it does—but it also engenders debilitating obfuscation, widespread confusion, and the potential for multitrillion-dollar fraud. Green portfolios are likely to underperform brown portfolios, according to research by Professors Robert Stambaugh and Lucian Taylor, colleagues of Henisz at Wharton.[12] Advocating green investments without prominent underperformance disclaimers almost certainly violates common fiduciary standards.

Over the course of his storied life, Sir Isaac Newton wrote more than one million words summarizing hundreds of experiments he conducted in secret, all in a vain search for "the philosopher's stone," a miraculous material that could transform iron to gold and wine to the highly coveted "elixir of life." Over more than four centuries, what he and his fellow alchemists ultimately discovered was multiple chemical compounds could be broken down into elements and then recombined.

ESG is no different. And just as alchemy eventually evolved into a valuable new field called chemistry, ESG may ultimately evolve into something more promising as well, something that verifiably promotes economic and social value creation simultaneously. What should it be called? Something less misleading and politically explosive than ESG, I hope.

Oh, just in case you were wondering, I was judged the debate winner. When presented with the facts, everyone agrees ESG's flaws must be fixed.

Notes

1. Terrence Keeley, "ESG Must Evolve into Something Less Politically Explosive Than ESG," RealClearMarkets, June 7, 2023, https://www.realclearmarkets.com/articles/2023/06/07/esg_must_evolve_into_something_less_politically_explosive_than_esg_903922.html.

2. *The Economist*, "3rd Annual Sustainability Week US," https://web.archive.org/web/20230603110435/https://events.economist.com/sustainability-week-usa.

3. Terrence Keeley, *Sustainable: Moving Beyond ESG to Impact Investing* (New York: Columbia University Press, 2022), 167.

4. UN Principles for Responsible Investment, website, https://www.unpri.org.

5. UN Department of Economic and Social Affairs, Sustainable Development, website, https://sdgs.un.org/goals.

6. Terrence Keeley, "ESG Does Neither Much Good nor Very Well," *Wall Street Journal*, September 12, 2022, https://www.wsj.com/articles/esg-does-neither-much-good-nor-very-well-evidence-composite-scores-impact-reports-strategy-jay-clayton-rating-agents-11663006833; and Zicklin School of Business/Baruch College, "The Difficult Truth About ESG Investing with Aswath Damodaran," YouTube, March 27, 2023, https://www.youtube.com/watch?v=8os1cmVXW0c.

7. Davidson Heath et al., "Does Socially Responsible Investing Change Firm Behavior?," *Review of Finance*, European Corporate Governance Institute, and University of Miami Business School, January 18, 2023, https://papers.ssrn.com/sol3/papers.cfm?abstract_id=3837706.

8. Terrence Keeley, "Vanguard's CEO Bucks the ESG Orthodoxy," *Wall Street Journal*, February 26, 2023, https://www.wsj.com/articles/vanguards-ceo-bucks-the-esg-orthodoxy-tim-buckley-net-zero-emissions-united-nations-initiative-nzam-f6ae910d.

9. Alex Edmans, "The End of ESG," *Financial Management* 52, no. 1 (Spring 2023): 3–17, https://papers.ssrn.com/sol3/papers.cfm?abstract_id=4221990.

10. Witold Henisz, LinkedIn, June 2023, https://www.linkedin.com/posts/witold-henisz-637584_esg-activity-7069766090016313344-u2K8/?utm_source=share&utm_medium=member_desktop.

11. Witold Henisz, LinkedIn, June 2023, https://www.linkedin.com/posts/witold-henisz-637584_sustainabilityweekus-whartonesg-climatechange-activity-7070088301377937408-kwmp/?utm_source=share&utm_medium=member_desktop.

12. Lubos Pastor, Robert F. Stambaugh, and Lucian A. Taylor, "Dissecting Green Returns" (working paper, Fama-Miller Center for Research in Finance, Chicago, June 10, 2022), https://papers.ssrn.com/sol3/papers.cfm?abstract_id=3864502.

A Primer on What a Fiduciary Shouldn't Do

Terrence Keeley

Wall Street Journal, August 1, 2023[1]

Asset managers, beware: Rep. Bill Huizenga (R-MI), chairman of the House Financial Services Subcommittee on Oversight, has sent letters of inquiry to BlackRock, Vanguard, State Street, Fidelity, and other firms before hearings scheduled for the fall on what it means to be a fiduciary.[2] "The lack of transparency surrounding the decisions asset managers make on behalf of millions of retail investors is concerning," he warns. "Congress must understand how asset managers fulfill their fiduciary responsibilities to prioritize financial returns and act in the shareholder's best interest."[3]

His committee likely will be deluged with legalese and financial gibberish to the effect that the asset-management business is much more complex than mere mortals could ever possibly comprehend.

For starters, different investors have different objectives and constraints—and there sure are a lot of different investors. On top of this, markets are hard to figure out. They go up and down, often more than common folks expect. Due to these vagaries, highly leveraged products make sense for some clients, while complex funds driven by arcane algorithms are the best fit for others. All responding managers will claim broad consumer choice is a social good and that they must offer a wide selection of products with an even wider set of fee structures to meet clients' evolving needs and goals.

Some clients choose to use Catholic or other social screens in addition to maximizing their returns. Does Congress dare think Catholics should be forced to compromise their principles? A growing number of mostly younger investors want their investments to "do well and do good." This means, in addition to beating the market, their investments are expected to benefit the least fortunate and stop raising the planet's temperature. Immediately. The idealism of these many young and other inexperienced investors' wishes has led hundreds of managers to offer trillions of dollars of ESG products.

Don't buy any of it. The asset-management industry thrives on two variables: margins and volumes. Its executives grow downright giddy when they can get both. Given an opportunity to sell plain vanilla index funds for a single basis point or more pricey ESG products that may or may not perform as hoped—well, need I say more?

Given that it will prove impossible for asset managers to explain succinctly how they pursue financial returns and operate in their clients' best interest, here are tips for Huizenga and his colleagues about how fiduciaries *don't* act.

No fiduciary allows clients to invest hard-earned money for unreasonable goals. No fiduciary allows clients to buy more expensive or riskier products when simpler, cheaper alternatives will do. No fiduciary hides costs or risks from clients. No fiduciary tires of listening to clients' objectives, even as markets and individual circumstances change. No fiduciary ceases educating clients about how others in similar circumstances have fared using different investing approaches.

Complete transparency with clients is a hallmark of true fiduciaries. That includes how a firm's stewardship team will vote clients' shares, which are owned by clients, not asset managers. This means clients' voices must be heard in boardrooms and during proxy fights—not the voices of their managers, who often have competing agendas. Almost invariably, asset owners want to maximize their long-run financial interests. More often than not, they don't want their investments spent on politics.

"In investing, you get what you *don't* pay for," John Bogle once wrote.[4] "Intelligent investors will use low-cost index funds to build a diversified portfolio of stocks and bonds, and they will stay the course. And they won't be foolish enough to think that they can consistently outsmart the market."[5]

Bogle died in 2019,[6] so Huizenga can't call on him to testify this fall. Still, let's hope Bogle's commonsense wisdom will prevail.[7]

Notes

1. Terrence Keeley, "A Primer on What a Fiduciary Shouldn't Do," *Wall Street Journal*, August 1, 2023, https://www.wsj.com/articles/a-primer-on-what-a-fiduciary-shouldnt-do-blackrock-vanguard-state-street-fidelity-investors-f1c2158.

2. Bill Huizenga, letter to Laurence Fink, July 18, 2023, https://huizenga.house.gov/uploadedfiles/2023-07-18_letters_to_asset_managers.pdf.

3. Bill Huizenga, "Huizenga Opens Inquiry into How Asset Managers Fulfill Their Fiduciary Responsibility," press release, July 18, 2023, https://huizenga.house.gov/news/documentsingle.aspx?DocumentID=402668.

4. John C. Bogle, "In Investing, You Get What You *Don't* Pay For" (speech, World Money Show, Orlando, FL, February 2, 2005), https://johncbogle.com/speeches/JCB_MS0205.pdf.

5. BrainyQuote, "John C. Bogle Quotes," https://www.brainyquote.com/authors/john-c-bogle-quotes.

6. Jason Zweig and Sarah Krouse, "John C. Bogle, Founder of Vanguard Group, Dies at 89," *Wall Street Journal*, January 17, 2019, https://www.wsj.com/articles/john-c-bogle-founder-of-vanguard-group-dies-11547677745.

7. Dawn Lim, "Five Ways Jack Bogle Changed the World of the Everyday Investor," *Wall Street Journal*, January 18, 2019, https://www.wsj.com/articles/five-ways-jack-bogle-changed-the-world-of-the-everyday-investor-11547815832.

Is ESG Profitable?
The Numbers Don't Lie.

Mike Edleson and Andy Puzder

Wall Street Journal, March 10, 2023[1]

Capitalists invest money, and manage companies, to do well financially. Proponents of so-called woke capitalism claim that companies can do "well" financially by doing "good" politically. The idea is that advancing a political agenda will also enhance profits and shareholder returns. Whether this does good is a matter of opinion, but whether it does well can be measured.

Woke capitalism makes its way into financial markets through an ill-defined concept known as environmental, social, and governance (ESG) investing. Huge investment managers use their ownership of shares to pressure companies to jump on the ESG train. But while individual investors are free to support whatever causes they wish with their dollars, those who invest other peoples' money have a fiduciary duty to focus solely on clients' financial interests. Thus, it's important to know whether politically focused companies actually do produce superior financial results.

To answer this question, we used research from 2ndVote Analytics, a company that scores US large-cap and mid-cap companies on their social and political engagement on a five-point scale.[2] The company evaluates company data on six social and political issues—the environment, education, abortion, Second Amendment rights, other basic constitutional freedoms, and support for a safe civil society—and generates a composite score. Company scores, updated quarterly, range from 1 (most liberal) to 5 (most conservative), with 3 meaning neutral or unengaged.

Roughly a quarter (or 221) of the S&P 900 large- and mid-cap companies studied scored 3—taking no political or social stance on any of these six issues—during the period from June 30, 2021 (when the data were first available), through January 31, 2023. Of the remaining companies, the political tilt was strongly to the left. More than 59 percent scored liberal and under 15 percent conservative (with only one company higher than 4).

We used a neutral score of 3 as a proxy for companies that focus on investors' returns rather than activism. We then compared the performance of those neutral companies with the market (represented by the S&P 500 and Russell 1000) and major ESG-registered funds. The point is to demonstrate how well a portfolio of business-focused politically neutral companies performs compared with those potentially distracted by political issues.

In making this comparison, we used a third-party index-calculation agent and market-value weighting in a manner similar to the S&P 500 and Russell 1000 benchmarks (total returns). The ESG products' returns include the effect of fees; the neutral-universe and benchmark indexes don't. The analysis covers the full period for which company scores were available, including the market run-up in the last half of 2021, the 2022 bear market, and the early 2023 rebound.

The results are compelling. The market was down overall, by 1.8 percent for the S&P 500 and 3.2 percent for the Russell 1000. ESG funds performed worse, with most losing 2.5 percent to 6.3 percent. A simple index composed of only neutral companies *gained* 2.9 percent, significantly outperforming both broad-market and ESG indexes in up and down markets. Notably, the benchmarks include the outperforming neutral companies—indicating that the politically active companies further underperformed.

We checked the robustness of this result in several additional analyses by varying the time frame (extending the index return calculation back five and 10 years) and the index construction (weighting). Across each time frame, the index of neutral companies significantly outperformed the S&P and Russell benchmarks. Essentially none of the performance difference could be attributed to sectoral composition or to how recently stocks were added to the indexes.

For a longer view, we compared the performance of the more than 200 companies that remained neutral over our data period with the benchmarks over the past 10 years. The neutral portfolio's cumulative return (334 percent) outgained the market (230 percent); the results were substantially more compelling using equal-weighted returns as an alternative method.

One interesting result is the point at which performance notably begins deviating—2017–18, around the time companies (and perhaps their profits and returns) began feeling pressure from the power and influence of supposedly passive asset managers such as BlackRock, State Street, and Vanguard, as those behemoths' push into ESG intensified.

The data indicate that, as common sense would suggest, companies that focus on profits outperform companies that don't. As a corollary, it seems obvious that asset managers won't maximize shareholder returns if that isn't their focus. It's hard enough to generate profits and returns when that is your focus, let alone when you're trying to change the world.

When the business of business is no longer business, it may be unclear who wins, but it's clear that shareholders lose.

Notes

1. Mike Edleson and Andy Puzder, "Is ESG Profitable? The Numbers Don't Lie," *Wall Street Journal*, March 10, 2023, https://www.wsj.com/articles/is-esg-profitable-the-numbers-dont-lie-benchmarks-analytics-politics-neutral-fiduciary-duty-market-woke-5da4a533.

2. Using the 2ndVote Analytics proprietary database of company scores for stocks in the S&P 1500 Index, the authors extracted all company scores (six scored issues per company) from the database for all stocks in the S&P 500 Index (large cap) and the S&P 400 Index (mid cap).

Columbia's "Woke" Investing Plan Would Imperil the Globe, Not Save It

Terrence Keeley

RealClearMarkets, July 7, 2023[1]

The year 2022 was a humbling one for ESG and the Paris agreement in particular. Along with destroying thousands of lives, Vladimir Putin's vicious assault on Ukraine shattered Europe's fictional energy security and countless livelihoods. As oil and gas prices skyrocketed, developed and developing countries alike found themselves engulfed by existential crises.

Then came a financial reckoning. Record numbers of investment funds that were underweight energy stocks underperformed their non-ESG counterparts by more than 1,000 basis points.[2] Only wise investors like Warren Buffett escaped the carnage; the best-performing stock in the S&P 500—Occidental Petroleum—happened to be one of Buffett's largest holdings, along with Chevron.

But humility is not a virtue in overabundant supply at Columbia University. Its Center on Sustainable Investment, an initiative jointly sponsored by Columbia's law and climate schools, just released a 68-page report, aptly titled *Finance for Zero*.[3] It brazenly champions one foolhardy idea after another, from how every human aspiration must be immediately sublimated to the 2050 net-zero goals to claiming finance's penultimate fiduciary responsibility is to attempt to regulate the earth's temperature.

It begins ominously: "As of 2023, the financial system is woefully misaligned with the world's climate goals."[4] Yet this is exactly what one should expect when global consumption and production patterns are equally misaligned, and no professional forecast sees a decline in oil and gas demand for the foreseeable future.[5]

Three countries—China, India, and Russia, the world's first-, third-, and fourth-largest emitters of CO_2 pollution—together now account for more than twice the greenhouse-gas emissions of Europe and North America combined.[6] (The US, at number two, emits less than half of China's carbon dioxide.) Getting the world aligned with the Paris agreement can happen only when these countries' leaders—Xi Jinping, Narendra Modi, and Putin—are as committed to net zero as Columbia insists the rest of us must be.

"Governments are responsible for producing official pathways," the Columbia report asserts, but "most of the world's regions lack a coherent . . . policy framework to achieve net zero by 2050, including guidance to financial institutions."[7] Only the second part of this tripartite claim is true: G7 energy and finance ministers, meeting recently in Sapporo, Japan, could not agree to put an end date on *coal* use, let alone oil and gas.[8] Yet telling financial institutions to realign their asset allocations to fictional energy pathways with no prospect for creation is the height of financial irresponsibility. Repeatedly exhorting pensioners to prioritize speculative environmental hopes above their all-too-real retirement needs violates basic fiduciary precepts.

Columbia at one point concedes that "short-term actions to decarbonize portfolios . . . may not be an effective way to support Paris alignment in the real economy."[9] But even this understatement shields a grave, inconvenient truth. Every sovereign wealth, pension, insurance, and institutional asset portfolio on earth could be aligned to net zero by 2050, and the world still would have no realistic chance to achieve balanced greenhouse-gas emissions by 2100. How so? There is more than enough private capital around to fund the rewarding investment opportunities like what Buffett seeks and routinely finds. If humans continue to consume oil, gas, and coal, capital will be found to produce them.

Finally, *Finance for Zero* exhorts all asset owners, managers, and banks to "shift new finance to activities that support the 1.5°C trajectory, which implies multiplying current financial flows to low carbon solutions by a factor of four to six."[10] This proposal is especially misguided. Decarbonization investments exceeded $1.1 trillion in 2022, the largest ever, and a jump of more than 25 percent versus 2021.[11] As the first law of economics (supply and demand) dictates, returns on said decarbonization investments dropped commensurately. Following the passage of Joe Biden's misnamed Inflation Reduction Act,[12] abundant government capital now vastly exceeds the supply of reasonably priced green investment opportunities. Columbia's insistence that lower-carbon investment rise to as much as $6 trillion per year, irrespective of investors' actuarial needs, reveals once more that liberal virtue broadly consists of generosity with other people's money.

It is the fiduciary responsibility of every asset manager to advise their clients about superior, real investment returns in their chosen time frames, not speculative ideas for a world a half century from now that some enlightened few contend would be better. This is exactly why Vanguard's CEO Tim Buckley recently withdrew from the Net Zero Asset Managers initiative,[13] an industry group that Columbia insists should be expanded dramatically. If investing for a better world happens to be an asset owner's priority, much more financing for low-income housing, drug-addiction care, minority-owned businesses, and charter schools should also be promoted. After all, our housing, education, health, and economic opportunity shortfalls today are at least as important as the possibility of higher temperatures a half century from now.

Energy security is economic and national security. Columbia's obsessions with the Paris agreement blind it to other human needs and irrefutable investment logic. At precisely the moment when ESG investing should be consigned to the dustbin of well-intentioned but failed financial paradigms, the Center on Sustainable Investment insists trillions be shoehorned into its preferred utopia, irrespective of cost.

Notes

1. Terrence Keeley, "Columbia's 'Woke' Investing Plan Would Imperil the Globe, Not Save It," RealClearMarkets, July 7, 2023, https://web. archive.org/web/20240106102657/https://themessenger.com/opinion/ columbias-woke-investing-plan-would-imperil-the-globe-not-save-it.

2. Lauren Foster, "The Best- and Worst-Performing ESG Funds of 2022," *Barron's*, November 17, 2022, https://www.barrons.com/articles/ best-and-worst-sustainable-funds-51668638595.

3. Lisa Sachs, Nora Mardirossian, and Perrine Toledano, *Finance for Zero: Redefining Financial-Sector Action to Achieve Global Climate Goals*, Columbia Center on Sustainable Investment, June 2023, https://ccsi. columbia.edu/sites/default/files/content/docs/Finance_for_Zero_CCSI_ June_2023.pdf.

4. Sachs, Mardirossian, and Toledano, *Finance for Zero*, 4.

5. Foster, "The Best- and Worst-Performing ESG Funds of 2022."

6. Andriy Blokhin, "The 5 Countries That Produce the Most Carbon Dioxide (CO2)," Investopedia, December 4, 2023, https://www. investopedia.com/articles/investing/092915/5-countries-produce-most-carbon-dioxide-co2.asp.

7. Sachs, Mardirossian, and Toledano, *Finance for Zero*, 7.

8. Motoko Rich, Lisa Friedman, and Jim Tankersley, "Behind the Scenes, G7 Nations Wrangle over Ambitious Climate Commitments," *New York Times*, May 20, 2023, https://www.nytimes.com/2023/05/20/ world/asia/climate-fossil-fuels-g7.html.

9. Sachs, Mardirossian, and Toledano, *Finance for Zero*, 14.

10. Sachs, Mardirossian, and Toledano, *Finance for Zero*, 9.

11. Nathaniel Bullard, "Clean Energy Investment Sets $1.1 Trillion Record, Matching Fossil Fuels for the First Time," *Time*, January 26, 2023, https://time.com/6250469/clean-energy-investment-sets-1-1-trillion-record-matching-fossil-fuels-for-the-first-time.

12. US Environmental Protection Agency, "Summary of Inflation Reduction Act Provisions Related to Renewable Energy," October 25, 2023,   https://www.epa.gov/green-power-markets/summary-inflation-

reduction-act-provisions-related-renewable-energy#:~:text=Most%20
provisions%20of%20the%20Inflation,%2C%20local%2C%20and%20
tribal%20organizations.

13. Terrence Keeley, "Vanguard's CEO Bucks the ESG Orthodoxy,"
Wall Street Journal, February 26, 2023, https://www.wsj.com/articles/
vanguards-ceo-bucks-the-esg-orthodoxy-tim-buckley-net-zero-
emissions-united-nations-initiative-nzam-f6ae910d.

The Progressive Case for Getting Rid of ESG

Alex Edmans

Wall Street Journal, August 19, 2023[1]

ESG is everywhere. It drives major strategic decisions at the world's largest companies, spurs the capital flows of leading asset managers, and dictates the core curriculum at prestigious business schools. Standard-setting bodies recommend the disclosure of a plethora of ESG metrics, and ESG-ratings firms each purport to offer the single best measure of a company's ESG credentials.

For advocates of ESG, this is a no-brainer: Decisions based on environmental, social, and corporate-governance factors, they say, can both improve financial performance and create societal value.

So let me say this as clearly as possible: ESG has outlived its usefulness. It's time we scrap the term.[2]

It isn't that I'm against integrating environmental, social, and governance considerations into decision-making. I've argued in favor of that myself,[3] and I'm widely viewed as an ESG advocate. But the infatuation with ESG has now gone too far. While an incorporation of ESG can enhance financial and social returns, an obsession with ESG can distract companies and investors from both objectives—by causing them to ignore non-ESG factors that may be even more relevant for long-term value.

Historical Coincidence

The special status given to ESG arose by historical coincidence rather than economic logic. The term was introduced by the 2004 United Nations report *Who Cares Wins*.[4] It promoted the UN Global Compact's 10 principles, which exclusively concerned social and environmental issues, and encouraged companies to adopt them in part due to their positive impact on financial results. The report quoted DuPont's chief financial officer as saying, "Every corporation is under intense pressure to create ever-increasing shareholder value. Enhancing environmental and social performance are enormous business opportunities to do just that."[5]

The previous year, a seminal academic paper was published showing that governance improves long-term shareholder returns.[6] It just so happened that investment researchers started recognizing the importance of "ES" to shareholder value around the same time, so the UN report brought the "ES" and "G" together—despite them being strange bedfellows. "G" typically ensures that a company serves its shareholders, whereas "ES" principally benefits stakeholders such as employees or communities. Even "E" and "S" may clash with each other; shutting down a polluting plant helps the environment but hurts workers.

If the key thread that ties ESG together is its financial significance, then there's no reason to exclude the many other factors that also create long-term value. In 1992, Robert Kaplan and David Norton introduced the "balanced scorecard,"[7] which highlighted how a company's value depends on not only its tangible assets but also its intangible assets. These include ESG issues, such as carbon efficiency and an inclusive culture, but also myriad non-ESG ones, such as strategy, productivity, innovation, capital allocation, and brand. None of them fall under the ESG label, but all are crucial for long-term performance.

Narrow Focus

Putting ESG on a pedestal above these other intangible assets can be damaging in three ways.

First, it narrows companies' focus. It causes them to give priority to components that have an ESG label attached to them over more important drivers of long-term returns—such as the elevation of superficial diversity statistics over genuine human capital development.[8] ESG then becomes a compliance exercise—a set of boxes to be ticked—rather than a framework to create value.

Second, it blurs companies' focus. They lose the ability to distinguish between the various items under the ESG umbrella, instead viewing them all as a homogenous mass of virtue. In 2011, I published a paper showing that companies with high employee satisfaction outperformed their peers over a 26-year period.[9] ESG advocates claimed that I'd proved that ESG works. But a study on employee satisfaction has no implications for other ESG issues, such as carbon emissions, animal rights, or water usage. Just because one ESG factor works doesn't mean you can blindly pursue another factor and hope to make money.

Third, it confuses companies. The halo around ESG leads them to think that it defies the laws of gravity—or at least the laws of economics. We often treat ESG metrics as if higher numbers are always better, but ESG is an investment and, like any other investment, exhibits diminishing returns. Trade-offs exist in almost every other area of economics, but some view ESG as a magic word for which the normal rules don't apply.

To be sure, ESG critics also make the same mistake of tarring all ESG items with the same brush—just from the other direction. Certain ESG factors have no link to performance, despite overhyped claims,[10] but this doesn't mean that other ESG factors can't pay off, such as governance and employee satisfaction. By attacking ESG indiscriminately, critics blind themselves to the possibility that *some* ESG issues *can* boost returns. It's ironic that some of the harshest opponents of ESG claim that companies' only purpose is to improve financial performance, when some ESG issues help with exactly that.

Societal Value

But what about the other argument for ESG—its societal impact? Many people believe that companies have wider responsibilities than simply making money and that ESG is the key to achieving those broader goals.

This argument ignores that non-ESG factors can also create substantial societal value. An innovative new product creates consumer surplus above and beyond the price paid for it. Productivity allows a company to create more with less, reducing resource usage and pollution emitted. Disciplined capital allocation prevents companies from wasting cash on executives' vanity projects, instead redeploying it to fuel the inventions of the future. Conversely, poor non-ESG performance can harm society. Kodak's sluggish executive team missed the digital revolution, eventually causing the company to go bankrupt and 150,000 employees to lose their jobs.

One could reasonably argue that the societal impact of some ESG issues, such as climate change, are even more important than non-ESG ones. But then these effects should be dealt with by regulation, such as a carbon tax, just like any other externality. Any substantial externality, ESG or not, should be dealt with primarily by the government. Just because one falls into the ESG bucket and attracts the attention of ESG investors doesn't give policymakers an excuse for inaction.

The Politicization

And there's another reason to scrap the "ESG" term entirely. The term has become heavily politicized, leading to ideological reactions rather than logical evaluations. Consider the following statements: "More ESG investment is always better" and "Considering ESG risks violates fiduciary duty." An ESG advocate will latch on to the former, and an ESG opponent the latter. But if we remove the word "ESG," we can assess the claims with a clear head. More investment isn't always better, due to diminishing returns, and taking risks into account is consistent with fiduciary duty—in fact, an essential part of fiduciary duty.

Instead of debating ESG, we should discuss "intangible assets" and "long-term value." Neither term is political, neither term excludes certain elements and puts a halo on others, and neither term leads to a cottage industry of consultants trying to ensure that something ticks a box. What matters is whether something improves long-term value, rather than whether it's called ESG.

The ESG movement had its time and place. It usefully drew companies' and investors' attention to the fact that nonfinancial factors can be financially material. But we've now known this for decades, and its time is past. Just as painting by numbers is useful for a child learning to paint but limiting thereafter, the current ESG-by-numbers approach has long outlived its purpose.

Let's scrap the politicized, simplistic, and restrictive term of ESG and free companies to create long-term value.

Notes

1. Alex Edmans, "A Progressive's Case for Getting Rid of 'ESG,'" *Wall Street Journal*, August 19, 2023, https://www.wsj.com/finance/investing/environmental-social-governance-investing-progressive-end-7ed70c34.

2. Alex Edmans, "The End of ESG," *Financial Management* 52, no. 1 (Spring 2023): 3–17, https://onlinelibrary.wiley.com/doi/full/10.1111/fima.12413.

3. Alex Edmans, *Grow the Pie: How Great Companies Deliver Both Purpose and Profit* (Cambridge, UK: Cambridge University Press, 2020).

4. UN Global Compact, *Who Cares Wins: Connecting Financial Markets to a Changing World*, 2004, https://www.unepfi.org/fileadmin/events/2004/stocks/who_cares_wins_global_compact_2004.pdf.

5. UN Global Compact, *Who Cares Wins*, 1.

6. Paul Gompers, Joy Ishii, and Andrew Metrick, "Corporate Governance and Equity Prices," *Quarterly Journal of Economics* 118, no. 1 (February 2003): 107–56, https://academic.oup.com/qje/article-abstract/118/1/107/1917018?login=false.

7. Robert S. Kaplan and David P. Norton, "The Balanced Scorecard—Measures That Drive Performance," *Harvard Business Review* (January–February 1992), https://hbr.org/1992/01/the-balanced-scorecard-measures-that-drive-performance-2.

8. Alex Edmans, Caroline Flammer, and Simon Glossner, "Diversity, Equity, and Inclusion" (working paper, European Corporate Governance Institute, Brussels, Belgium, August 22, 2023), https://papers.ssrn.com/sol3/papers.cfm?abstract_id=4426488.

9. Alex Edmans, "Does the Stock Market Fully Value Intangibles? Employee Satisfaction and Equity Prices," *Journal of Financial Economics* 101, no. 3 (September 2011): 621–40, https://www.sciencedirect.com/science/article/abs/pii/S0304405X11000869.

10. Alex Edmans, "Is There Really a Business Case for Diversity?," *Medium*, October 30, 2021, https://medium.com/@alex.edmans/is-there-really-a-business-case-for-diversity-c58ef67ebffa.

About the Authors

Phil Gramm is a former chairman of the Senate Banking Committee and a nonresident senior fellow at the American Enterprise Institute.

Terrence Keeley is the chairman and CEO of 1PointSix and the Impact Evaluation Lab and the author of *Sustainable: Moving Beyond ESG to Impact Investing* (2023).

Mike Edleson is a retired chief risk officer of the University of Chicago's endowment and the former chief economist of Nasdaq and the National Association of Securities Dealers.

Alex Edmans is a professor of finance at London Business School and the author of *Grow the Pie: How Great Companies Deliver Both Purpose and Profit* (2020).

Hester Peirce is a Securities and Exchange Commission commissioner.

Andy Puzder is a former CEO of CKE Restaurants, a distinguished fellow at the Heritage Foundation, and a senior fellow at Pepperdine University. He is the author of *The Capitalist Comeback: The Trump Boom and the Left's Plot to Stop It* (2018) and *A Tyranny for the Good of Its Victims: The Ugly Truth About Stakeholder Capitalism* (forthcoming).

Mike Solon is a partner of US Policy Metrics.